INSIDE JOHN DEERE

A FACTORY HISTORY

ROD BEEMER AND CHESTER PETERSON JR.

MBI Publishing Company

DEDICATION

For some of the many who helped us by setting our skittish feet more firmly on life's path: Kurma Moline, Elbert Macy, Chester Bruce, Dr. Louis Holland, Dr. R. F. Fountaine, Dr. G. B. Marion, Leonard Bishop, Dr. Charles V. Dorothy, and Pat LoBrutto.

First published in 1999 by MBI Publishing Company, 729 Prospect Avenue, PO Box 1, Osceola, WI 54020-0001 USA

© Rod Beemer and Chester Peterson, Jr., 1999

MBI Publishing Company books are also available at discounts in bulk quantity for industrial or sales-promotional use. For details write to Special Sales Manager at Motorbooks International Wholesalers & Distributors, 729 Prospect Avenue, Osceola, WI 54020-0001 USA.

Library of Congress Cataloging-in-Publication Data

Beemer, Rod.
    Inside John Deere: a factory history /Rod Beemer & Chester Peterson, Jr.
        p. cm.
    Includes index.
    ISBN 0-7603-0441-6 (pbk.: alk. paper)
    1. John Deere tractors--Design and construction.
    2. Manufacturing processes.
    3. Deere and Company--History.
        I. Beemer, Rod.
        II. Title.
TL278.P48   1999
338.7'6292252'0973--dc21   98-32353

On the front cover: A 1997 model 7210 has completed much of its journey down the assembly line at Deere & Company's Waterloo, Iowa, Tractor Operations. The 7210 came equipped with a Deere & Company-built 6.8-liter Powerteck diesel engine rated at 95 PTO horsepower.

On the frontispiece: The 4450 wasn't introduced until 1983, but this model was no doubt completed years before the real tractors were introduced. The model shop, as well as the engineering department, has to work well in advance of actual production. In even the smallest detail, this model looks about as real as the big models.

On the title page: The Deere & Company Administrative Center in Moline, Illinois. President Bill Hewitt's vision that led to the construction of this complex helped redefine Deere & Company's image as a progressive worldwide leader in the industry. The original structure was completed in 1964, and a west wing (on the left) was added in 1978.

On the back cover: Top: Six-cylinder engine blocks on the line at Deere & Company's Engine Works in Waterloo, Iowa. These units were in production in June 1997 and will provide power for some future Deere & Company agricultural tractor or combine. Although the Engine Works is highly automated, there are a few jobs that require the skill of experienced technicians to get the job done right.

Bottom: The Deere & Company's Gold Key program allows customers to accompany their tractors down the assembly line while they are built. Upon completion, the customers use the gold key to start their tractors and drive them off the assembly line. This Gold Key customer is receiving the key to his new 8200 John Deere in October 1996. The 8200 was built from 1994 to 1997 and produces 180 PTO horsepower.

All photography and illustrations provided by Deere & Company
Designed by Tom Heffron

Printed in China

CONTENTS

ACKNOWLEDGMENTS

The primary source for information about Deere & Company is Deere & Company. Employees, past and present, are the "company." Without the cooperation of Deere & Company's retired and current employees, this book wouldn't have been possible.

These people have earned both our respect and gratitude for their cooperation and help: Jim Doyle, product manager, Trademark Administration; Don Morgenthaler, Corporate Communications; Gordon Tjelmeland, Corporate Communications; Renate Zerngast, Visual Services Department; Rand Tapscott, Visual Services Department; Don Duncan, manager, Waterloo Tractor Operations; Beth Bader, Visitors' Services, Engine Works; Gretchen Nesteby, Visitors' Services, Engine Works; Bob Payne, Visitors' Services, Tractor Operations; Ted Abkes, Visitors' Services, Tractor Operations; Mike Mack, retired director, Product Engineering Center; Harold Brock, retired director, Product Engineering Center; Les Stegh, archivist; Paul Knedler, manager, Visitors' and Special Services; Waldean Grauerholz, retired manager, Product Tests and Evaluation; Mike Friedman, Distribution Center; Bill Bulow, retired, Waterloo Foundry; Khalil Kingsbury, retired general manager of North American Foundries; Gary L. Brogan, Overseas Division, Region 1; David C. Everitt, Overseas Division, Region 1; Warren Wiele, retired engineer and inexhaustible source of Deere history, information, and "war stories"; and Chuck Beemer, artwork.

We also want to express thanks to everybody else who helped us fashion the background for this book.

INTRODUCTION

However humble the beginning, nothing can fire hopes, dreams, and ambitions like hanging one's name above the door of a business and placing one's name on a product. It has been said that there is no greater high than launching a successful business. When he opened his first blacksmith shop in Leicester, Vermont, in 1829, John Deere most likely experienced such a rush.

When Deere fired his forge in the pre-dawn hours and began putting iron to anvil, he began to grow a successful and profitable business. He pursued his vision with extraordinary drive and perseverance. However, in his most sublime dreams and grand plans, he couldn't have envisioned the scale, depth, and prominence Deere & Company would attain 170 years into the future.

Neither John Deere nor his son Charles lived to see the name "John Deere" on a tractor. Yet today the "John Deere" nameplate is attached to tractors produced and used around the world. Deere & Company is the name "over the door" of the company that's become the world's leading manufacturer of agricultural equipment. From a humble blacksmith shop, Deere & Company has grown into a massive global corporation that conducts business in 160 countries and employs 33,900 people. Its factories and offices can be found in almost every corner of the world.

A work such as this has to be focused and has some inherent limitations. Otherwise, an encyclopedic book would be the result. This book devotes considerable coverage to the company's agricultural tractor works, engine works, and foundry at Waterloo, Iowa, because it is representative of most Deere & Company factory facilities, regardless of country.

Our hope is that this book will pay tribute to the dreams of one man and document the ingenuity, persistence, and hard work of the individuals that have made John Deere the company it is today. Their achievements and successes are truly outstanding.

A BLACKSMITH BUILDS AN EMPIRE

JOHN DEERE'S PIONEERING PLOW BUSINESSES AND FIRST FACTORY

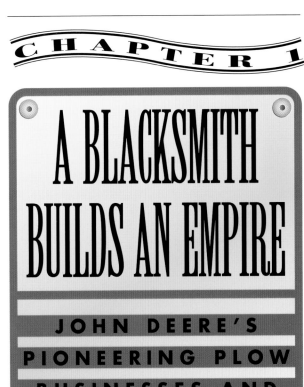

escribed by acquaintances and friends as "crude," a "hard taskmaster," and "very Yankee," John Deere, the founder of Deere & Company, was a man driven to succeed. As the following pages will tell, despite many setbacks, Deere always gave his all and expected the same from those around him.

A favorite Deere & Company tale that has been passed down through the ages demonstrates Deere's unrelenting drive to create his products and provides insight into his personality. One day, Deere was following one of his employees as the workman was carrying plows down a stairway in the factory. This worker wasn't moving fast enough for Deere, so Deere gave him a push causing him to fall down and injure himself. The work-

An artist's rendering depicts John Deere in his blacksmith shop working with hammer and anvil. No doubt it was in a shop much like this in Grand Detour, Illinois, that he built his first steel plow.

man was down, but he wasn't out. In fact, he was so angry he chased after Deere. But Deere ran and successfully escaped his pursuer. According to lore, John didn't run from cowardice but rather out of shame. Later, he asked a trusted employee to go find the worker and smooth things over.

The remarks of a former partner of Deere's, John M. Gould, made while testifying at a trademark infringement case in the mid-1860s, provide further insight into the mind and inner workings of John Deere, the man, depicting him as a hard-working rather than creative individual. Gould stated, "I should not call him a man of general inventive ability. The improvements he would make would be by practice or experimenting more than creative or inventive."

Despite, or perhaps because of his "taskmaster" ways, Deere triumphed brilliantly, leaving behind a remarkable legacy. The company he founded is the only major farm equipment manufacturer that hasn't been sold or merged into a giant conglomerate. For fiscal year 1996, Deere & Company was 119th on the Fortune 500 list of the largest U.S. industrial corporations. Deere also won *Fortune* magazine's "most admired" award in the farm equipment and industrial category.

In sharp contrast to the success, prominence, and prestige of the present day, the path to the top for Deere & Company was filled with extreme peaks and valleys.

JOHN DEERE'S VERMONT ROOTS

The story of Deere & Company really starts in the early 1800s, with the birth of its founder John Deere. On February 7, 1804, to be exact, Sarah Yates and William Rinold Deere became the parents of a son, John, born in Rutland, Vermont.

William Deere and his wife are commonly thought to be Welsh immigrants; however, John Deere stated that both his father and mother were born in England. Perhaps Deere didn't make a distinction between Wales and England since both are part of Great Britain. Common belief is that his mother was the daughter of Captain James Yates, a Revolutionary War veteran. He wasn't one of the patriots, but instead a Redcoat who stayed stateside after the fighting ceased.

By 1806, William and Sarah Deere and their five children were living in Middlebury, Vermont, where William plied his trade as a tailor. In 1808, he sailed for England in hopes of receiving an inheritance to help put his family on firmer financial footing. Tragically, he

John Deere's operation evolved from a shop to a small factory at Grand Detour, Illinois. His steel plows became so popular that additional help was essential.

never returned. John was only four years old when he lost his father. It is unclear what happened to William Deere, but the cold hard truth was that the family lost its head of the household and breadwinner.

DEERE EMBARKS ON A BLACKSMITHING CAREER

Out of immediate need, John's schooling became a second concern. Deere was expected to assume a big role in assisting the family to survive. It wasn't unusual that children helped support their families during the trying days of the pioneering era, especially in single-parent families. Survival meant helping with the numerous daily chores and earning a few cents whenever possible. As was the practice of many youths of the day, Deere signed on as an apprentice to a journeyman tradesman—in his case, a blacksmith. History doesn't define the circumstances or motivation for the decision.

Was it a family decision arrived at with counsel from his mother and siblings, or did Deere make the decision strictly on his own? The answer remains unknown.

And why blacksmithing? Why not tailoring like his father? Perhaps Deere realized that his deceased father's trade hadn't been monetarily kind to the family. What other trade would be in great demand during the coming years? The village smithy was indispensable to a community, providing services to virtually every household, farm, and business in the area. All kitchens needed pots, pans, and skillets. Working horses (and in this era all horses worked in one form or another) required horseshoes. Wagons and buggies needed ironwork.

William Deere had moved his family from Rutland, Vermont, to Middlebury, Vermont, in 1806, and they stayed there after his disappearance. It was in Middlebury where John Deere embarked on a black-smithing career that would eventually change the world. From 1821 to 1825, Deere apprenticed at various local

John Deere's reconstructed blacksmith shop at the John Deere Historic Site in Grand Detour, Illinois. This site was located and excavated by a professional team of industrial archaeologists from the University of Illinois.

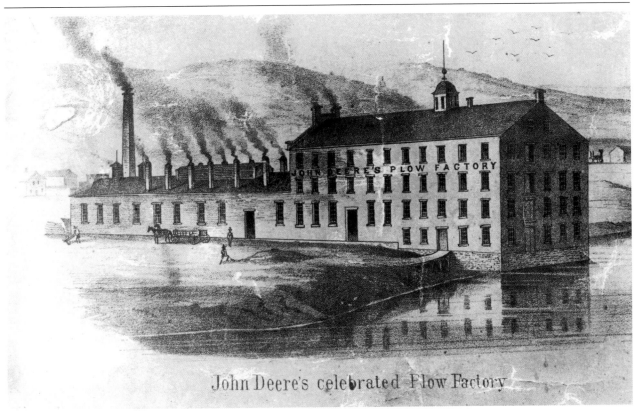

"John Deere's celebrated Plow Factory" is the caption on this drawing of Deere's facility in Moline, Illinois.

shops. After completing his apprenticeship, he was hired as a journeyman by two different blacksmith shops.

Deere's work was good enough to catch the eye of Colonel Ozias Buel. He proposed that Deere move to Colchester Falls, Vermont. He suggested Deere open a blacksmith shop there that would serve the community as well as produce ironwork for a sawmill and a linseed-oil mill that Buel owned. Deere provided the valuable ironwork service for Buel's mills, but he didn't stay long. In 1827, Deere married Demarius Lamb, daughter of William and Mary Lamb of Hancock, Vermont. The couple immediately moved to Vergennes, Vermont, north of Middlebury. John and another local black-smith, John McVene, worked together for a short time.

DEERE OPENS HIS FIRST BLACKSMITH SHOP

In 1828, the couple moved to Salisbury, Vermont, where a son, Francis Albert, was born. Most likely, Deere worked for one of the two blacksmith shops in town or at the Briggs Shovel Factory. Just two years later, the Deere family was living in Leicester, Vermont. At this location, John embarked on another of his many ventures as a shop owner. He purchased some land and built the very first John Deere facility, a small crude wooden structure. The term "facility" didn't accurately

describe the small structure. A more appropriate label would be "shop." In actuality, it was a one-man shop. However humble the beginning, it was a beginning, nonetheless. Unfortunately, it was a beginning fraught with disaster and hardship.

This venture lasted little longer than a well-banked forge fire. Almost immediately fate dealt him a harsh blow—the new enterprise, his first shop, was destroyed by fire. He wasn't going to give up easily. He doggedly rebuilt the shop only to have another fire destroy the second structure as well. Deeply in debt, he was forced to sell the property three months after he bought it. In addition, the responsibility of a second child, daughter Jeannette, was added to his life. To provide for his family, Deere was forced to seek work as a journeyman in Royalton, Vermont. Deere found employment repairing the many stagecoaches, wagons, and coaches that traveled the local roads. In 1832, Deere had another addition to his family. Daughter Ellen Sarah was born.

The Deere family moved again in 1833, and this time the destination was Hancock, Vermont. Once again Deere gave up the security of employment for the pursuit of the American dream. Although still in debt from his Leicester venture, he was able to secure enough property to build both a home and a blacksmith shop. Here another daughter, Frances, was born.

ARMY OF WORKMEN AT DEERE & CO.— MOLINE.

A virtual army of Deere & Company men work at one of the company's facilities in Moline, Illinois. It gives us a glimpse into the industrial world of the past. However, there are two questions that beg answers: Is the barefoot boy in the first row an employee, and what's the subject and significance of the picture around the neck of the worker in the second row? This photograph was probably taken around the turn of the 20th century.

A railcar of walking plows is ready for shipment in 1882. Deere's decision to move to Moline, Illinois, gave him access to rail transportation that made delivery of his products much easier and faster.

Charles Deere took every opportunity to get out in the field and work with the company products. Here he's giving a "hands-on" plowing demonstration in 1905.

INTERIOR OF FORGE SHOP.

INTERIOR·OF GRINDING SHOP.

INTERIOR VIEWS OF DEERE & CO., MOLINE PLOW WORKS, MOLINE, ILL

These are interior views of the forge and grinding shop at the Moline Plow Works. The overhead drive-line furnishes flat-belt power to the floor machinery.

An early photograph from the Deere & Company archives is believed to be of this Hancock blacksmith shop. It had approximately the same dimensions as a large two-car garage. Small, yes, but no doubt it was an object of pride and the realization of a dream come true for John Deere. Unfortunately, outstanding debts continued to plague the family. Jay Wright, who had loaned the money for Deere's original blacksmithing venture in Leicester, was becoming both impatient and insistent about repayment.

Deere just couldn't seem to get the debt paid off. Wright went to the courts for action, and the courts obliged with a writ that was served on Deere in the fall of 1836. The 32-year-old John Deere decided that fleeing to the West, leaving his family and business, was the only payoff for 15 of hard work blacksmithing. Deere took another big risk when he left, but starting fresh without the shadow of old debt was critical. There was no way for him to know what his hasty escape would bring him. It would ultimately provide the setting and opportunities needed to bring him success, fame, and fortune.

DEERE ENGINEERS A SUCCESSFUL BUSINESS

In 1837, Deere traveled to Grand Detour, Illinois, and planted his stakes. Amos Bosworth, an acquain-

tance of Deere, may have enticed Deere to come to Grand Detour. In addition, Bosworth's son-in-law, Leonard Andrus, a prominent businessman, was the original settler of Grand Detour in 1835. Bosworth was Deere's former employer in Royalton, Vermont. Two different accounts exist concerning Deere's available cash when he arrived in Grand Detour. One is that he had $1,100 with which to begin his new life, a not inconsiderable sum for the times. The second view is that his pocket contained a mere $73.73. As Deere sold his Vermont blacksmith business for all of $200, it seems unlikely that the $1,100 figure is realistic.

Regardless of his financial status, Deere rented land and constructed a building for his blacksmith shop during his first summer in Grand Detour. It was his fourth blacksmith shop in six years. Here he once again fired up his forge and began to hammer out a new business venture. By 1837, the first Deere factory built in Grand Detour was completed. It measured 26 feet wide by 53 feet long—only 1,378 square feet.

In his new facility, Deere offered all the services performed by the village blacksmith. These "bread and butter" jobs included shoeing horses, repairing kettles, and sharpening tools, as well as a host of other repair jobs to keep merchant wagons rolling and farmers' implements field-ready. Additional income was provided

This military limber and caisson was made by Deere & Company for the war effort during World War I.

These Douglas engine assemblies were built by Deere & Company female employees during the war effort. Note the "RESTRICTED" stamp on the image. This photograph was taken in 1944 and has since been removed from the restricted files.

by "manufacturing" pitchforks, shovels, and other products, which he personally took to merchants throughout the community.

Deere didn't have a monopoly on the blacksmith trade; other men were following the same pattern of operation. However, Deere's products were soon recognized for their unsurpassed quality. From this point on, Deere began to transform his business operation from that of a tradesman to that of a manufacturer.

Helping to revolutionize both Deere's immediate and future business was the fabrication of his first plow utilizing a steel saw blade. Even though the steel plow didn't originate with Deere (as is commonly thought), his plows scoured well in the wet, sticky soil of the midwestern prairie, and they soon sold equally well. (Records state that he sold three steel plows in 1839.)

Back in Vermont, a son Charles was born in 1837 after Deere's departure for the West. His wife and family finally joined him in 1838.

Soon thereafter Deere embarked on a series of partnerships in his quest to grow and diversify. One of his first jobs at Grand Detour was to mend the broken pitman shaft on Leonard Andrus' sawmill. The two men

soon entered into an informal business arrangement. By 1842, Deere acquired 160 acres of land on the Rock River where water power could be applied to the machinery of a new factory. Although debt still plagued Deere, between the two partners they were able to construct a two-story factory on the property.

When the new building was completed, the business moved from Deere's original shop to the new facility two blocks away. An advertisement from that time shows the new factory with the name "L. Andrus Plough Manufactory." Records indicate that 100 plows were manufactured and sold in 1842. The next year production quadrupled to approximately 400 plows. In 1843, the two men altered their business arrangement into a formal partnership, agreeing that the business would be operated under the name, "L. Andrus." This partnership dissolved in 1848.

A MONUMENTAL MOVE TO MOLINE

Deere then sought a new location for his factory as the railroad was bypassing Grand Detour. He needed a new factory that would have rail access to get materials in and products out. Deere's choice for the location of his next business was Moline, Illinois. In addition to railroad facilities, the town was located at the then-important confluence of the Mississippi and Rock Rivers.

The location offered what Deere was looking for. Making use of the town's extensive transportation facilities proved to be a sound business decision. Deere's professional and private life had taken a long, winding, and arduous road, and his life of constant changes was coming to an end. This final of Deere's many physical plant moves lasted not only for the rest of his lifetime but has endured for more than a century and a half. John Deere had found a permanent home in Moline.

However, the move didn't result in the last of Deere's partnerships. He immediately signed an agreement with Robert N. Tate. The name over the door read Deere & Tate. The company name didn't last long. John Gould joined the budding partnership and added his name to the venture, forming Deere, Tate & Gould.

In mid-September 1848, construction of the new factory was completed and was up and running almost immediately. By the end of the month, the partnership had built and sold 10 plows. Thus, a period of rapid growth and strong sales began. According to the sales records of early 1849, it's apparent that the products Deere and partners were producing were meeting a vital need in the surrounding communities. As the settlers moved into the area, plows to break the virgin land were in high demand. According to Robert Tate's records, the following numbers of plows were

A couple of railroad cars are loaded with John Deere tractors in 1992. Through its history, Deere and Company has relied on rail shipment to reach customers.

manufactured: January, 255; February, 215; March, 194; April, 301; and May, 235.

A two-story addition was built onto the existing structure adding 4,800 square feet to the existing 1,440 for a total of 6,240 square feet of manufacturing floor space. In 1852, the company structure was altered once more. Deere's daughter Jeannette married an attorney, James Chapman, who joined the partnership. Tate and Gould left the partnership in 1853, and Deere's son Charles joined the firm.

Manufacturing continued to soar. More models were added, and the number of implements rose dramatically. During 1857, *The Cultivator* printed Deere & Company's production numbers: 800 large breakers, 1,300 small breakers, 9,000 stubble plows, 1,000 corn plows, 300 Michigan double plows, 100 double- and single-shovel plows and cultivators, and 900 other items. This 12-month total of 13,400 units represents a most respectable monthly production of some 1,116 implements.

DEERE & COMPANY UNDER NEW LEADERSHIP

Deere sold out his interest to his son-in-law Christopher Webber in 1858. On paper, 21-year-old Charles Deere and Christopher Webber owned the entire company. Stephen H. Velie, who married Charles' sister Emma in 1860, joined the company in 1863. The firm was again reorganized in 1868 and incorporated as Deere & Company with Deere and his son Charles as equal partners. What happened to Webber's and Velie's interests isn't known. This act, at last, brought to an end to the many and varied partnerships in which John Deere had participated over a span of 47 years.

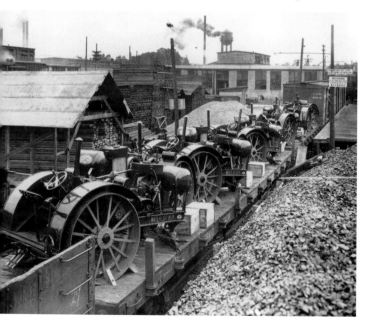

Waterloo Boys are ready for rail transport in 1920. Note that some things haven't changed all that much when compared to the image of 1992 tractors on a railcar 72 years later.

The Union Malleable Iron Company located in East Moline, Illinois, looked like this in 1919. The factory provided castings for Deere & Company products.

Original shareholders of Deere & Company are listed as John Deere, Charles Deere, Stephen Velie, and George Vinton. One year later, Charles V. Nason and Gilpin Moore joined the original four as stockholders. The new corporation's first few years could rightly be called the "foundational" years of the growing company. It exhibited a strong record of production and had enough history to give it direction. Charles was listed as the president, yet there's no doubt that John was still quite active in the company. He made sure that much of the "character" that he'd instilled into the organization continued to be maintained.

However, Charles took firm command of the company and implemented several policies that established Deere & Company as one of the leaders in the manufacture of farm implements. One such policy involved distribution. As production and demand increased, it became obvious that the distribution network needed to be significantly improved. A product isn't any good if the company can't get it to the farmer without undue complication and expenditure of time.

Up until the late 1850s, sales and distribution for almost all companies of that era were handled by traveling salesmen or travelers. These men peddled their firm's

Originally the Moline Wagon Company of Moline, Illinois, the firm was purchased by Deere & Company in 1911, becoming the John Deere Wagon Company. One of the largest in the world, it could produce 30,000 wagons a year.

products from town-to-town and even from farm-to-farm. The local merchant, the "dealer" who handled a manufacturer's product, had little or no ties to the company. And usually the merchant had the option of selling just one item or a full line. A merchant could sell a competing manufacturer's wares, guided only by his business interests.

In 1869, Charles Deere broke new ground and opened the first Deere & Company branch house, and it was followed by four more during the next two decades. The branch house concept tied the marketing organization to the parent company either as a wholly owned subsidiary or through other financial or management arrangements. This way the manufacturer, Deere & Company, possessed a marketing arm of the business that was tied to its line of implements. In actuality, it was in a sort of "partnership" with the manufacturer.

By making this move, Deere & Company continued its tradition of customer service excellence. Charles Deere had placed a strong emphasis on marketing and sales that would be a trademark throughout his career. The upshot: Deere & Company could now provide a full-line and full-service dealership for the benefit of farmers. In retrospect, this may have been one of the most significant moves of many that Charles Deere contributed to the company.

Charles recognized his father's drive and impatience to get the job done in the factory, but the younger Deere differed from his father and exercised extreme patience in product development. Stephen H. Velie, brother-in-law and close confidant of Charles Deere, said, "Sometimes a good deal of money is made by taking great risks, but it seldom happens that any honor or profit comes to a manufacturer in bringing a new departure or anything not proven comparatively profitable. . . . We have always been cautious of too radical changes and of new implements. . . ."

DEERE & COMPANY ENTERS THE TRACTOR MARKET

By the turn of the century, tractors, a major development in farm power, were added to the lines of many farm implement manufacturers. Company after company furiously rushed to market tractors. Deere & Company took a different approach. It followed a tried and tested as well as cautious and conservative approach. It waited, evaluated, and let others spend time and money on research and development.

Nevertheless, it wasn't long before the company's own branch house dealers were clamoring for a tractor to complement the full line of Deere & Company equipment. Some were even bold enough to include a competitor's tractor in their catalogs. Both Case and International Harvester were heavily promoting tractor

Built in 1912, the East Moline Harvester Works marked the company's entrance into the harvesting machinery field. During that first year 2,000 harvesters—binders—were produced. In 1913, corn binders were added to production, and in 1914, mowers and sulky rakes were placed into production.

A plow like this could make even the stoutest team of horses faint! Actually it was built by Deere & Company in 1879 for the Iron Mountain and Southern Railroad and was used for track ditching. The plow was hooked to a flat car and pulled by two locomotives.

research and development. A growing number of farmers began looking to these manufacturers for their other farm implements too.

Deere & Company responded on two fronts. In 1912, Deere included the Twin City Model 40 tractor in its export literature to Argentina and Uruguay, and at the same time, the Deere & Company board of directors decided to develop a tractor plow. C. H. Melvin was given the job of producing the first experimental model. One tractor was built, which was a three-plow, three-wheeler. Development on this tractor stopped in 1914.

That same year, Joseph Dain Sr. was instructed to produce a tractor that could be sold to farmers for approximately $700. The Dain All-Wheel-Drive tractor was the first production tractor to bear the John Deere name. The first tractor was a success, but in a ironic twist of fate, neither John Deere nor his son Charles Deere lived long enough to see a John Deere tractor plow a field.

Following the production of the first Dain tractor, Deere & Company again took the conservative path of careful testing, pricing, and studying the competition. Orders were issued in 1917 to build 100 of the Dain tractors. However, in early 1918 Deere & Company bought the Waterloo Gasoline Tractor Company. The decision (consistent with past company expansion efforts) had been to research the best available and add it to the Deere & Company line through some sort of acquisition.

The Waterloo Boy tractor was modified through several model changes. The Waterloo Boy name was retained until the famous Model D John Deere was adopted for production in 1923. It was the progenitor of the green two-cylinder tractors that soon became recognizable all over the world.

It was in the post–World War II period that farmers found they needed a tractor for nearly every job on their farms. In the late 1940s and early 1950s, farms continued to get larger, which in turn resulted in a need for ever more powerful tractors and the implements to go with them. The New Generation line of four- and six-cylinder tractors was unveiled in 1960, and two years later Deere & Company surpassed International Harvester to become the world's leading farm equipment manufacturer.

Deere's dream that began in a shop in Vermont, a "factory" in Grand Detour, Illinois, and a true manufacturing facility in Moline, Illinois, grew and grew and continues to thrive today.

CHAPTER 2

DEERE & COMPANY'S EPICENTER

THE WORLD HEADQUARTERS AT MOLINE

From the time that John Deere moved his company to Moline, Illinois, it has served as company headquarters. Decisions that determined the fate and direction of Deere & Company were made at 1325 Third Avenue in downtown Moline from 1870 until 1955. But the company needed room to grow and reach its potential.

A GROWING COMPANY ON THE MOVE

In 1955, a new office building was built at 3300 River Drive. Although it was considered a new beginning, it wasn't Deere & Company's corporate home for long.

An array of Deere products proudly stands on the display floor of the Administrative Center. Also visible on the right wall is the renowned 180-foot-long "mural" created by artist Alexander Girard.

23

it wasn't Deere & Company's corporate home for long. CEO Charles Wiman had died, and Bill Hewitt became president and CEO. Under his leadership, the company took a new direction. He had his own specific plans for Deere & Company, and one of those plans was to give the corporate headquarters a look that signified its history, future, and prominence in worldwide business. Hewitt had a vision for a majestic, grand, exquisite new building complex for the company.

In 1956, Hewitt began searching for an architect to build the future home of John Deere, and in January 1957, the board gave authorization for a new headquarters. Hewitt hired renowned architect Eero Saarinen. Saarinen's international reputation for impeccable work had preceded him. He had designed the auditorium at the Massachusetts Institute of Technology, the General Motors Technical Center, and the St. Louis Gateway Arch. The two scouted the area around Moline for a fitting location. A site three miles south and four miles east of the former downtown Moline offices was selected after all downtown locations were rejected.

Hewitt's vision of Deere & Company's new Administrative Center is best stated in a passage from Wayne G. Broehl Jr.'s book *John Deere's Company*:

> At the start, Hewitt laid out a comprehensive "letter of intent" for the architect, making clear that the building design "will be in harmony with our functions and additions and also be indicative of the objectives and progress that we envision for the future."

> Hewitt characterized the men who had built the company as "rugged, honest, and close to the soil," men who had always put a central emphasis on "quality of product and integrity in relationships with other persons." Inasmuch as "the farmer wants and needs the most efficient and durable tractors and implements," therefore "we also want and need a headquarters building that will utilize the newest and best architectural and engineering concepts." Hewitt concludes, "The several buildings should be thoroughly modern in concept but should not give the effect of being especially sophisticated or glossy. Instead, they should be more 'down to earth' and 'rugged.' "

AN ARCHITECTURAL MARVEL IS CREATED

To make Hewitt's vision a reality, Saarinen's design incorporated the use of exposed external steel frames.

The display floor at the Administrative Center could well serve as a genealogy of Deere products. The Froelick tractor, with red flywheels, is situated in the background, and the famous John Deere steel walking plow sits in the right foreground.

These exposed frames weathered and "rusted" to a predetermined degree, giving the exterior of the building a rich patina. As one employee observed, "It matches the bark of the trees." It's so in harmony with the surroundings that the building appears to rise out of the ground rather than "sit" on the landscape. The rust factor led some to refer to the complex as the "rusty palace." And the use of "rusty" metal prompted at least one long-time employee to comment, "For years we've warned farmers about the harmful effects of rust. Yet here we are with an administrative building constructed of rusty metal."

In 1964 the building opened. The complex is part university campus from the immaculately kept grounds, part government grounds because of the imposing size, and part museum because of the numerous art objects displayed. It sits on 600 landscaped acres on John Deere Road in Moline. Around the building are 50 acres watered by underground sprinkler systems and two man-made lakes featuring lighted fountains. Another distinguishing feature of the building itself is an interior atrium in the building's center so that offices on all sides overlook the gardens.

In 1978, a new west wing was added. Saarinen's successor, Kevin Roche, complemented the original facility by connecting the wing via a fourth-level corridor-bridge. Both the Administrative Center and the west wing addition won the *Administrative Management* magazine's "Office of the Year" award.

THE ADMINISTRATIVE CENTER

The Administrative Center complex (which covers 800,000 square feet) houses the corporate offices. In addition, the advertising department, supply management, visual services, engineering, and other support services occupy the building. Approximately 2,000 full-time and contract employees comprise the Administrative Center staff. The building offers three cafeterias, and an auditorium that seats 350 people serves as a meeting place for corporate functions. It also hosts certain community events. Visitors can view the display floor and auditorium from 10:30 A.M. to 2:30 P.M., Monday through Friday. Over the years it has hosted U.S. presidents and foreign heads of state, as well as such personalities as Muhammad Ali.

This is an aerial view of the Deere & Company Administrative Center at Moline, Illinois. The complex resides on 600 acres of land three miles south and four miles east of the downtown area.

Deere & Company founder, John Deere (1804–1886). He served as corporate president from 1869 to 1886. His steel plow of 1837 was the foundational implement that eventually led the company to worldwide prominence as a farm implement manufacturer. Although John Deere didn't actually invent the steel plow, it was his insistence on quality and his marketing strategy that made it successful.

Charles Deere (1837–1907), son of John Deere. He served as corporate president from 1886 to 1907, making two very important contributions to the company. First, his financial savvy turned the company around after he joined it in 1858. Second, he introduced the concept of the branch house, which gave Deere & Company its outstanding marketing system.

The main entrance of the Administrative Center is a glorious and fascinating tribute to Deere & Company past, present, and future. When visitors enter, they immediately recognize that they have arrived in "Deere territory." A cross section of John Deere products is on display inside the main entrance. The display is periodically changed, so visitors have a chance to examine new and different equipment. This includes lawn care equipment, industrial equipment, antique implements, new agricultural tractors as well as antique tractors.

On the back wall is a glass-enclosed display area featuring an 8x180-foot-long mural by artist Alexander Girard. The work was described as a three-dimensional historical mural. This is a good description, although not technically accurate in the strictest sense. This historical mural shows items from the company's past, and it captures the essence of a dynamic era of our rural heritage and of Deere & Company. One must see this piece of art in person to fully appreciate it.

John Deere's history and industry involvement are richly captured in this impressive display. More than 1,000 objects associated with John Deere and his company are attractively displayed. These items include advertising posters, photographs, historical documents, and a vast amount of other enthusiast paraphernalia. Each piece provides a valuable perspective on farming culture, American society, and rural living from 1869 to the present. In a certain sense, these are symbols of America's past. In the early part of the century, a high percentage of the population lived and worked on farms. During the Great Depression,

William Butterworth (1864–1928) married Charles Deere's daughter, Katherine Deere. He was corporate president from 1907 to 1928. Butterworth's family had roots in Virginia, but his father served as U.S. representative from Ohio in the 1870s and 1880s. Butterworth held a law degree from the National University Law School in Washington. It was under Butterworth's watch that the company expanded to a full-line company by purchasing several manufacturing firms. He also shepherded the company through the introduction of tractors and combines, World War I, and the Great Depression.

many Americans migrated to the cities looking for work; this era in U.S. history transformed the makeup of the nation. So visitors to the Moline Administrative Center are essentially looking through the glass at a time capsule.

SENIOR MANAGEMENT'S HOMEBASE

Although Moline headquarters is a popular tourist and tractor enthusiast destination, as well as an architectural triumph, this building is used to manage and guide the vast Deere & Company worldwide empire. Many of the decisions that have guided Deere & Company to unparalleled heights have been made in the offices and boardrooms of this building. Deere & Company is a dynamic changing corporation, and management changes along with the evolving company. Future success hinges on the people at work in the administrative center. The current management staff includes Hans Becherer, chairman and CEO; Joseph England, senior vice president, finance and accounting; Robert Lane, senior vice president and managing director Europe; John Lawson, senior vice president, engineering, technology, and human resources; Bart Bontems, vice president, industrial relations; Wade Clarke Jr., vice president, government affairs; Frank Cottrell, vice president, general counsel, and corporate secretary; Mertroe Hornbuckle, vice president, human resources; Nathan Jones, vice president and chief financial officer; William R. Hubbard Jr., vice president, quality; Curtis Linke, vice president, corporate communications; R. David Nelson, vice president, worldwide supply management; James Robertson, vice president and comptroller; and Robert Wismer, vice president, engineering. All work out of this building.

DEERE'S DECENTRALIZATION STRATEGY

Throughout Deere & Company's history, the company has successfully addressed and handled the issue of decentralization/centralization. This management and coordination or tug-of-war between headquarters and satellite facilities has been ongoing since Deere & Company began buying companies. The issue has been a part of boardroom debates for decades. Although a complex situation, by definition the company is decentralized. To understand how this relates to the management of a plant such as the Waterloo Tractor Works, Don Duncan, Manager, Waterloo Tractor Operations, was asked: If you wanted to design and build a new tractor would you have to check with Moline? "Only in the respect that they fund it," he responded. "We're decentralized but not that decentralized," is his reply that helps put the issue into perspective.

THE VISITOR SERVICES PROGRAM

They come from all over the world—students, farmers, and just plain vacationers with no connection to agriculture. Regardless, they all share a common interest in Deere & Company's high profile as a world leader in agricultural and industrial manufacturing. And they all want to have a first-hand view of Deere & Company.

Deere & Company recognizes this interaction with the public as part of its business. The Visitors' Services Department at the Moline headquarters employs eight full-time personnel plus numerous contracted retired

Charles Deere Wiman (1892–1955), grandson of John Deere and corporate president from 1928 to 1942 and 1944 to 1955. (Burton F. Peek was president from 1942 to 1944 during Charles Wiman's service in the U.S. Army.) Wiman made the final decision to end the era of the two-cylinder tractor that had been a long-time hallmark of Deere & Company.

Deere employees, bringing the staff for this department to more than 50. All employees receive structured training to ensure that they're knowledgeable about the products and the processes. As new products or new processes are introduced to the manufacturing floor, the Visitors' Services guides undergo additional training so the information they give on tours is both correct and current.

The Visitors' Services program expects to guide 30,000 visitors through the Waterloo Tractor Works in 1998. The Engine Works anticipates 12,000 interested visitors in 1998. The Waterloo Foundry sees roughly the same number as the Engine Works. The Harvester Works at Moline sees approximately 25,000 to 30,000 visitors annually. Tours are also given at other Deere & Company North American plants and some overseas facilities. However, numbers aren't currently available for these locations. Beth Bader of the Engine Works Visitors' Services observes that the most often-heard comment she hears after people take a tour is how impressed they are with the cleanliness of the facility.

A STUNNING TRIBUTE TO DEERE'S HISTORY

The John Deere Pavilion is drawing droves of visitors to downtown Moline. The building was constructed to preserve and celebrate John Deere's history, tradition, excellence, and quality. But this isn't just any building, this is a majestic 14,000-square-foot glass and steel visitor or enthusiast center located on John Deere Commons near the site of the first plow factory John Deere built in Moline. This glass and steel cathedral is a monument to John Deere's manufacturing history and its involvement in feeding the world. Farm vehicles and implements that marked milestones in John Deere history are on display here.

The Pavilion was built in response to increasing requests of the public to tour Deere & Company's manufacturing facilities. As an example, the current interactive "combine display" allows Pavilion visitors to take a factory tour of the Harvester Works without going through the actual facility. When the Pavilion opened on August 16, 1997, approximately 35,000 people attended the grand opening and ribbon cutting ceremony. As of May 12, 1998, more than 150,000 people had visited the Pavilion. And adjacent to the Pavilion is the John Deere Store, where the enthusiast or fan can find memorabilia, collectibles, and a wondrous variety of products.

FUTURE "BEGINNINGS"

There have been many milestones in the Deere & Company story. Are there major milestones for agriculture and the "tools of the trade" in store for the future? Going back four decades and highlighting a few of the major developments of John Deere tractors may whet your appetite for what may lie ahead.

In 1960, Deere & Company unveiled the New Generation of Power. This represented a major step in gear design, closed-center high-pressure hydraulics, and operator comfort, not to mention the shift from two-cylinder to four- and six-cylinder engines. Then, in 1962, came the power-shift transmission. It allowed shifting between gears on-the-go without using the clutch. In 1972, the Sound-Gard body was introduced to provide a level of comfort unprecedented in tractor history. Four-wheel-

William A. Hewitt (1914–1998) married Patricia Deere Wiman. He was corporate president from 1955 to 1964 and CEO from 1964 to 1982. Hewitt was the last of the Deere family to serve as chief executive of Deere & Company. His career had numerous highlights, but introducing the New Generation tractors, establishing a strong presence in the global market, reaching number-one rank as an agricultural machinery producer, and the new Administrative Center are perhaps most prominent.

drive articulated models became production tractors in 1974. They soon became common in farming operations around the world.

A few years later, in 1978, came the mechanical front-wheel-drive that allowed the front wheels to be driven from the rear differential. At about the same time, electronic control of many functions blossomed, with advancements such as implement-to-hitch interfacing and electronic-controlled fuel injection. Today, electronics is a significant part of total "vehicle" control. Global Positioning System (GPS) is currently being adapted to tractors for use in tailoring fertilizer applications and planting rates to varying field conditions and soil analysis results.

All right, if you were to do a "Rip Van Winkle" and wake up in 20 years, would you recognize a tractor if you saw one? The jury is still out on this question. For instance, Harold Brock, retired Deere & Company engineer, answers, "I think you would." On the other hand, Don Duncan, manager, Waterloo Tractor Operations, quickly replies with a "no."

FINANCIAL STATUS

Incidentally, in 1998 (the same year that this book is being written) Deere & Company will almost certainly exceed $1 billion net income for the first time! Approximately 61 percent of its net revenues will be from sales of agricultural equipment, 21 percent from sales of construction equipment, and 18 percent from sales of commercial and consumer equipment. Including Financial Services revenues, roughly 78 percent of revenue is from U.S. and Canadian sales, 21 percent from overseas sales, and 1 percent from other revenue sources.

JOHN DEERE FACTORY LOCATIONS AND ENGINEERING CENTER

The following is a listing of major John Deere equipment manufacturers worldwide as of 1996:

AGRICULTURAL EQUIPMENT

Arc-les-Gray, France: Balers, forage equipment, and materials-handling equipment

Bruchsal, Germany: Tractor and combine cabs

Des Moines, Iowa: Cotton harvesting, tillage, planting, and spraying equipment

East Moline, Illinois: Combine harvesters

Horizontina, Brazil: Agricultural tractors, combine harvesters, and planting equipment

Madrid, Spain: Components

Mannheim, Germany: Agricultural tractors

Moline, Illinois: Planting equipment and hydraulic cylinders

Monterrey, Mexico: Tillage tools and cultivating equipment

Nigel, South Africa: Agricultural tractors and tillage equipment

Ottumwa, Iowa: Hay and forage equipment

Saltillo, Mexico: Agricultural tractors

Waterloo, Iowa: Agricultural tractors, product engineering, foundry, and major components

Welland, Ontario, Canada: Materials-handling equipment and rotary cutters

Zweibrucken, Germany: Combine harvesters and forage equipment

INDUSTRIAL EQUIPMENT

Davenport, Iowa: Construction and forestry equipment

Dubuque, Iowa: Construction equipment

Kernersville, North Carolina: Deere-Hitachi

Construction Machinery Corporation—hydraulic excavators

Saltillo, Mexico: Backhoes, excavators

COMMERCIAL AND CONSUMER EQUIPMENT

Augusta, Georgia: Commercial utility tractors

Columbia, South Carolina: Saw chain

Enschede, The Netherlands: Commercial riding mowers

Gastonia, North Carolina: Hand-held power products

Greenville, Tennessee: Walk-behind mowers and lawn tractors

Greer, South Carolina: Hand-held power products

Gummersbach, Germany: Walk-behind mowers

Horicon, Wisconsin: Lawn and garden equipment

Knoxville, Tennessee: Commercial products

Raleigh, North Carolina: Commercial, golf, and turf mowers

Welland, Ontario, Canada: Utility vehicles

DEERE POWER SYSTEMS GROUP

Coffeyville, Kansas: Power transmission equipment

Dubuque, Iowa: Engines

Rosario, Argentina: Engines

Saran, France: Engines

Saltillo, Mexico: Engine assembly

Torreon, Mexico: Engines

Waterloo, Iowa: Engines

PARTS DISTRIBUTION CENTERS

Bruchsal, Germany

Milan, Illinois

Robert Hanson (1924–), CEO, 1982–1990. Hanson assumed the company presidency in 1978 after a career at Deere & Company that included wide leadership experience in the international arena. What faced him in 1982 as CEO was a severe recession/depression in the agricultural machinery business. The fact that Deere & Company survived while other agricultural machinery manufacturers faltered is noteworthy of his leadership.

Hans W. Becherer (1935–), CEO, 1990–present. Born in Detroit, Michigan, he is a graduate of Trinity College, Hartford, Connecticut, and the Harvard Business School. In 1987, Becherer became president and chief operating officer of Deere & Company. He was named chief executive officer in 1990 and assumed the role of chairman of the company's board of directors the following year. In 1996, his responsibilities were expanded to include those of chief operating officer.

DEERE'S ENVIRONMENTAL INTEGRITY

Deere & Company doesn't intend to ignore the environment either, one of the hottest topics in the eyes of its customers and potential customers. A recently revised corporate environmental policy reaffirms the company's goal for excellence and continuous improvement with respect to overall waste reduction and environmental responsibility. The objective: to reflect the company's strong commitment to developing a sustainable environment while stressing integrated environmental considerations into overall business-planning processes throughout the world.

"We're clearly the industry leader in most environmental aspects," CEO Hans Becherer emphasizes. "Deere & Company's policy will ensure that our environmental efforts support our corporate goals of profitable growth and continuous improvement."

A COMMITMENT TO EMPLOYEE SAFETY

Another concern of the company and its employees is safety. Exemplifying Deere & Company's excellent safety record in its facilities is the number of commendations its various units have received recently. Eight Deere & Company units received the Iowa-Illinois Safety Council awards for outstanding performance in 1997: Davenport Works, Dubuque Works, Engine Works, Harvester Works, Ottumwa Works, Waterloo Works, Seeding Group (Moline), and Parts Distribution Center (Milan, Illinois).

Regardless, there's much assurance based on past history that whatever the next decades bring in agricultural equipment design there's no doubt that Deere & Company will continue its position in the vanguard.

EVOLUTION OF THE JOHN DEERE TRADEMARK

Numerous artists' renditions of the deer theme have been used by John Deere and his company. Some depicted a deer's head and antlers; some show the deer in a stately pose, but it is the leaping deer that has appeared in all registered trademarks used by the company since 1876. These seven show the evolution from 1876 to the present.

Beginning with this registered trademark in 1876, the leaping deer has appeared in all Deere & Company trademarks.

In 1912, this version of the leaping deer trademark was adopted.

Introduced in 1936, this was the shortest-lived trademark of Deere & Company.

This trademark was issued in 1937, the same year Deere & Company celebrated its 100th anniversary.

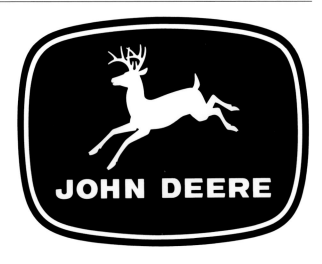

The "MOLINE, ILL." was dropped from the 1950 rendering of the trademark. Perhaps this was in anticipation of the company's growing participation in worldwide markets.

This trademark was featured on Deere & Company products in 1956.

Deere & Company was the undisputed industry leader when this trademark was introduced in 1968.

ENGINEERING TOMORROW'S TRACTORS TODAY

THE PRODUCT ENGINEERING CENTER

The Product Engineering Center (PEC) is John Deere's equivalent to the Pentagon's War Room. In both cases, these are the facilities where the next "campaign" is planned. Specifically, the PEC is where engineers create, develop, and research new components, systems, and products. The result is an ever-expanding array of agricultural products.

While almost every enthusiast would like to peek into these secret inner sanctums and get a glimpse of the future, the opportunity is not afforded to mere mortals. The PEC is directly tied to John Deere's future prosperity. The entire PEC is off limits to most people other than PEC employees.

This is the Product Engineering Center (PEC) undergoing a renovation and an addition in 1981. The first PEC shop building was built in 1954; offices were added in 1956, and the complex was fully occupied in 1976. This is the place where future John Deere products are created.

Moreover, the pattern and model shop is top secret. To drive the point home, retired PEC director Mike Mack said he couldn't even get his wife clearance to view the model shop.

Although the Product Engineering Center spearheads John Deere's research and development efforts, it isn't the only facility conducting product development. To keep on the leading edge of each of the industries that it serves, John Deere spends over $1.5 million *per day* on R&D. This includes all the R&D conducted at the PEC and other engineering locations.

The PEC, the Deere & Company center for worldwide product design control, is housed in a building located on a slight rise above a small man-made lake. The multistoried brick and glass front offices overlook the sparsely developed south edge of Waterloo, Iowa. The eye-catching complex and test facilities reside on a 1,000-acre parcel of land that has been home to the PEC since 1956.

ENGINEERING TEAMS

One group works on the chassis of the vehicle. The tractor group designs and develops the operator's platform and entire station (including the seat, the location of the pedals, and the levers), the enclosures, all the styling pieces, the hood shape and profile, the radiator mounting location and size, oil coolers, all the controls, and the ergonomics of the vehicle. The tractor must be designed around the end user—the farmer. This group goes to great lengths to make the tractors as comfortable, attractive, and user friendly as possible. If a design is fatiguing or uncomfortable, something has failed during the design and development process. However, as indicated above, John Deere has taken numerous steps to virtually eliminate that possibility. It has a reputation for building some of the most comfortable tractors around.

Another group of engineers is responsible for developing entirely new powerplants or modifying existing engines. Current production engines are upgraded to meet the increasing requirements for more horsepower and better fuel efficiency, or to satisfy a particular demand of the marketplace.

The transmission group is faced with the task of engineering a more efficient transmission while maintaining an unparalleled level of durability. A better, more powerful engine is of little value unless that power is efficiently transferred from the engine to the axles.

Past tractor and implement innovators such as Henry Ford and Harry Ferguson transformed the industry. Both Ford and Ferguson had a burning passion to design a tractor system that would transfer farming from human muscle to mechanical muscle. Innovations such as the three-point hitch, remote hydraulic cylinders, and power steering have made Ford and Ferguson's passionate pursuit a reality.

The PEC, likewise, thrives on innovations, performing extensive research and development to bring them to fruition. Their goal is to push these concepts, components, and products to the edge. While working to realize maximum performance, they strive also to maintain the highest level of reliability. In turn, customers are afforded the best product possible. As farming methods change, the hydraulic systems on a vehicle must be changed and improved to keep pace with new demands. In addition, new revolutionary systems such as onboard computers and GPS (global positioning systems) have been incorporated on Deere tractors in recent years. This is the result of years of development by John Deere's engineering groups, especially those at Deere & Company's PEC.

Non-engineering groups at the PEC include the accounting department, where part-by-part and assembly-by-assembly costs are computed to determine product costs. In addition, there's the important matter of operational cost, so the expense to run the PEC is also part of the accounting function.

The procurement or purchasing department is part of the PEC staff and is responsible for either outsourcing or having fabricated at least 4,500 major components that go into the building of a tractor. In the case of experimental or prototype units, this can sometimes include scores of individual parts that make up components.

In addition, the PEC maintains its own personnel department to staff the various departments. The total number of employees has ranged from 900 to 1,700 over the past two decades.

The machine shop and its personnel are also a very important part of the PEC. The machine shop is responsible for all experimental parts for prototype products. While the machine shop has all the capabilities necessary to put a tractor together and make it work, what it actually does on-site comes down to economics, availability, and delivery date. Some parts are machined on-site in the facility, while others are outsourced. If an engine block is desired, it comes from the foundry. Then it could be possibly machined at the PEC, or it could be machined at an outside source.

TESTING

Spend some time at a farm sale, country church, or co-op and you'll meet many retired farmers who wear hearing aids or say "what" frequently. The thousands of hours farmers spent on unrefined tractors in the 1930s, 1940s, and even 1950s was a major contributing factor to this loss of hearing. On most models, there were few provisions to guard against the engine and tractor noise. Noise level testing at the Deere PEC is a sophisticated process. Noise tests are conducted to standards that have been developed in the industry.

As an example, the industry determines the position and distance where the testing microphone must be placed in relation to the operator's ear. The test operator sits in the cab with a microphone mounted to his or her helmet. With the operator inside the cab, the noise level is measured over the complete range of different power levels. This is performed in a controlled soundproof room with a dynamometer hooked to the vehicle. Extensive research and development of Deere Sound-Gard enclosures dramatically reduced noise levels for the operator. In fact, noise levels have been reduced to the level of current automobiles.

Besides noise-level tests, the PEC conducts several other industry-standardized tests, including Roll-over Protective Structure (ROPS) tests and pendulum tests (the latter to be detailed below). Deere & Company engineers were deeply involved in helping establish these tests, which are standards in the industry.

The pendulum test is a severe impact test. A huge steel pendulum weighing several thousand pounds is suspended above the test unit. When it is released, it swings down and strikes the enclosure from the back. This test is also repeated to impact the cab from the side.

All of the test parameters are precisely stipulated in the industry standards test. Specifically, the weight and vertical distance the pendulum is raised before being released are stated. Of course, the higher the pendulum is raised before it's released, the more energy that is transferred upon impact on the enclosure.

While the industrial equipment division uses similar pendulum tests, they also conduct an impact test on the front of the enclosure. A front rollover in an industrial environment is a common hazard, which is why the pendulum test is also done to the front of the industrial units. Agricultural vehicles aren't tested from the front because it is extremely rare for this vehicle to incur a frontal impact or a front rollover. On these vehicles, the blow from the rear and sides measures the relative protection the operator has from the tractor rolling over backwards or sideways.

COMPUTER-AIDED DESIGN AND MANUFACTURING TECHNOLOGY

Of course, drafting tables and drafting tools have long ago been replaced by computer monitors and keyboards. The role of computers is substantial, and computers are

By 1981 when this image was taken, the computer age had fully arrived at the Product Engineering Center (PEC) in Waterloo, Iowa. Besides providing design capabilities, computers are used in testing products even before the field testing is begun. Drawing on past data, the computers can predict many failure modes before they happen.

integrated into nearly every function of the PEC. Mike Mack said, "There are lots of different applications for computers; in fact, computers run the whole show today."

As early as 1956, the PEC began utilizing computers. Initially, they were used as a better way to perform mathematical analysis of stresses and strains. Before the introduction of computers, metal strength analysis was calculated manually. Then, in 1956 or 1957, computer programs were written to assimilate information and speed up the engineering process.

Another preliminary use of computers by Deere & Company was in the design of the geometry of the gear teeth. Before computational analysis had to be done

manually. Bearing durability, torsional shaft vibration, axle shaft stress, transmission shaft stress, and the deflection of the transmission shaft were calculated with pencil and paper.

"When I was designing gears as a young engineer," Mack recalled, "I'd spend several days on designing one gear mesh. When the first computer program came along, it did the thing in 15 minutes. Now computers do it in 15 seconds or less."

In 1980, computer-generated graphics were instituted. All designs, systems, and components are now created with Computer-Aided Design (CAD) software. Engineers create a component or product with the CAD

A transmission is undergoing rigorous testing and computer analysis in a test cell at the PEC circa 1988. All relevant data is being collected, compiled, and outputted by the computer system.

program and transfer the file to the appropriate manufacturing machines—a Computer-Aided Manufacturing (CAM) station that interprets the information from the CAD file and outputs the product.

Another application of computer technology is Computer Numerically Controlled (CNC) machining in which the computer actually drives the cutter path of a cutter. Numerous CNC machines are used by Deere & Company, including plasma cutters that cut parts from sheet metal and lathes that turn the specified part.

Mack puts the application of computers as applied to design and testing into perspective: "The computers do a lot better job and are much more reliable than manual computation," he said. "If you were trying to balance the stress between a pinion and a bull gear, you might manually go through the calculations two or three times, maybe four times before you have a stress balance. It still wouldn't be really balanced, but you'd be closer to being balanced. With a computer you can run dozen and dozens of iterations in a matter of seconds. And when it's all through, the stress will be exactly balanced. Computers give a hell of a lot better product." Computer precision allows much more power to be produced by the engine and transmitted by the transmission. But the engineer's mandate is still the same: design new products as well as redesign and improve existing models.

CUSTOMER AND MARKET RESEARCH

With more than 40 years of experience at Deere & Company, Mike Mack has worked as an engineer at the old Moline Tractor Works and the Dubuque Tractor Works, and he was director of the PEC at Waterloo for 17 years. When asked where one starts to build a new tractor, Mack explained, "It all starts, of course, with the customer. The engineering group and the marketing group work in tandem to put their fingers on the pulse of the customer. They have to establish some sort of product definition, and this is quite different in various parts of the country. And to make the whole problem much more complex, Deere & Company is a global organization. This means that you have to go way beyond just the local market, and obviously, each one of these areas has varying requirements that are unique to its region."

Mack continued, "There are differences in the crops; there are differences in Deere & Company plant management conditions; there are differences in available resources in terms of suppliers; there are differences, strong differences, in cultures as you go from one country to the other. The balancing act, then, is to try to fold as much commonness in as you can in order to control the total machine tool investment. But at the same time, you have to be quite sensitive to the local requirements, and so that's where the balancing comes in."

Although most owners and operators climb on their machines without contemplating how their tractors were designed and engineered, the vehicles and products are specifically designed to suit the specific needs of a particular group of operators.

One of Deere & Company's methods of keeping abreast of customer needs dates back to John Deere himself. Deere went out into the field and asked the farmer what he needed and then supplied a superior product. Mack said, "A most important part of the whole process of establishing the early specifications is interacting with our people in the field. Now this has to be done with a certain amount of care because when you go to the field you talk to dealers and farmers, asking, 'what do you think we need in the next line of tractors?' They think in terms of technology that's known to them, existing technology. They don't have in mind technology that the engineer has in mind. Meanwhile, the engineer is looking down the road six or eight years and has a lot of technology and innovation that he can envision and has access to, of which the dealer and the farmer may not have an understanding at the time. So the engineer has to fold in the technology that's coming down the pike with what the customer demands or requests."

MANY INVOLVED IN THE PLANNING PROCESS

To maximize a product's chance at success, Mack said many departments are involved from the inception of the product, manufacturing personnel included; their involvement helped ensure that product design didn't create excessive cost or produce manufacturing difficulties.

According to Mack, "Manufacturing folks are brought in early, because their input will influence much of the nature of the design itself. This whole organizational structure has evolved over the years and changed over the years but always with a similar pattern. There are people in Moline, Illinois, who do some product planning. But let me go back 10 years. We had a product planning group of 15 to 20 people who worked with the product engineering group in Waterloo, Iowa, which, at the time of my retirement in 1987, had an organization of approximately 900 people. In the heydays of 1970 to 1981, we had a peak employment in the Product Engineering Center of roughly 1,700 people. Each model would have a certain engineering staff working on that model. And from within that group, [there] would be 8 or 10 people involved in what I'd call product planning. They would be working with the folks in Moline getting different dealers and customers together."

Mack continued, "Then as those plans evolved, they'd start to create the specifications and some of the preliminary specs. As the project grew, the number of people applied to the project would grow as well. In the end, of course, we'd have everybody working on the project. The planning process is a whole continuum of activities as part of the planning process. You stay with it all the way into production."

THE MANUFACTURE OF PRODUCTS

Deere & Company is a global company, and often several plants around the world produce the same component. Engines are made in Waterloo, Dubuque, France, Spain, and Mexico. How Deere & Company coordinates production and supply capacity is a point of interest. Mack explained, "Some of the engines made in Saran, France, are the same as the engines made in Dubuque. However, the engines that are made in Waterloo aren't made in France or Dubuque. But the exchange of engines and components is influenced by exchange rates. The currency exchange rates fluctuate from time to time, and, of course, that has a significant influence on what is exported and imported.

"In addition to cost of production, these factories also have different capacities. If the demand in one area is less than the demand in other areas and the differential can be compensated for because of the differences in capacity, then that's a consideration in deciding where the engines or other components will be outsourced."

Mack expanded on the topic, "For years Deere & Company was considered to be more vertically integrated than most other tractor companies. By vertically integrated, I mean Deere & Company made its own components. And Deere & Company probably made more of its own components for many [more] years than any other tractor company in the world. In recent years, though, you're seeing more outsourcing of components. Again, this is purely a matter of economics. If something can be outsourced for less money and is dimensionally compatible, it's the economical thing to do. This is the reason all companies attempt to arrive at standardization.

"Let's take, for example, where a flywheel housing will interface with an engine block. The more standardization that a company can arrive at in the dimensions of where the bolt holes are located, the more standardization it has. And the more opportunity it has to supply those engines to a variety of vehicles and tractors."

A model utilizing 90 percent of existing components and tooling can be manufactured in a relatively short time frame. Depending on the magnitude of the specification change, or upgrade, according to Mack, the timeline for a "new" model could range anywhere from 18 months to 5 years. Producing a completely new model, a model that is new from the ground up, is a different story. The last time Deere & Company released an entirely new tractor was in 1960 when the New Generation tractor was released. It was a 7-year project from inception to the production line.

Mack adds that a definitive time frame for manufacture is almost impossible to determine because of all the factors that must be considered.

NEW GENERATION TRACTORS

The New Generation model holds a distinct honor within Deere & Company. In the history of the company, there has never been anything as drastically different from previous models in product design. It was different in every single respect. The entire hydraulic system, featuring a closed-center hydraulic system, was totally new. The steering system was a new concept. It was the first tractor that had no mechanical link between the front wheels and the steering wheel—the only link being a hydraulic line. The planetary final drive system was completely new to Deere & Company, which had never built such a system up until that time. Obviously the engine was new. Deere had never before built a multicylinder engine for tractors.

Today, all the subsequent John Deere tractor models have planetary final drives, and all tractors have engines based on the original New Generation design. These four- and six-cylinder engines were made in 1960 when the company switched from the two-cylinder design. This design technology has been carried over from the 1960 New Generation to all the "descendent" tractors built today. All tractors that have been brought on-line are essentially improvements of these early tractors. All the engineering and design time on those original tractors has since been applied to and benefited all subsequent tractors.

All of this technology was developed after the Deere & Company PEC started operation in 1956. At the time, it was under the direction of Merlin Hansen, who many consider the father of the New Generation tractors. The team of engineers included various key people. Design of these tractors was managed by Wally Dushane and development by Don Wielage. Key designers included Sid Olsen, engines; Vern Rugen, transmissions; Danny Gleeson, chassis and controls; Ed Fletcher, hydraulics; and Chris Hess, hitch.

WORLDWIDE TRACTORS

A huge step in tractor design and later implement design was put in place two years after the introduction of the New Generation tractors. In 1962, PEC ushered in the "worldwide" concept that would influence subsequent Deere & Company models.

Retired Director of PEC Harold Brock remarked, "Our next program was to design a worldwide tractor at Waterloo. Dubuque made one kind of tractor; Mannheim,

Germany, was making tractors of another design; and both of these differed from the concept of the 3020, 4020. So we said we need a worldwide tractor, one that will satisfy the world. Deere & Company was accused by many other countries of designing a tractor primarily for the Blackhawk County, Iowa, area. With that in mind, we brought the engineers from the different Deere & Company factories to Waterloo."

Brock went on to say, "Then we sat down and planned what would satisfy their market as well as the United States market. Our purpose was to determine what kind of a product would be best for markets on a worldwide basis. That's when the 1020, 2020 series was developed. That was a rather unique experience; it kind of set the standard for the world.

Brock continued, pointing out some of the difficulties that had to be overcome: "If you machined a part from our United States prints in Germany, it would turn out to be the 'opposite hand,' or reversed. We realized we needed a drawing that wouldn't have to be converted.

The finishing touches are applied to a model of the 4450 tractor. Not many people get a peek into the model shop at Waterloo's PEC. That's because this is where the concepts of future tractors take shape as scale models.

Under the system then used, when they converted our inch/decimal system into millimeters/metric, they had to round off the numbers. That meant precision parts didn't always fit because their dimensions couldn't be rounded off evenly. We set out to make a drawing that wouldn't have to be redrawn and from which any factory in the world could make the part from it. This was the start of our worldwide concept of drawings. Germany and the other countries agreed to use our projection for the drawing format.

"We simplified the concept further by using symbols on the drawings instead of notes in German, French, Spanish, or Italian. If a part had to be round or square or linear, you wouldn't be reading it; you'd instead see a symbol. Then we decided to design in even millimeters and also put in the odd decimal equivalent. Whatever machine with which somebody was working, either inch or metric, the part could be machined from the print without converting. In addition, all materials specified on the drawings were in even metric numbers, ensuring that all gauges were the same throughout the world. That was the start of the Deere & Company worldwide design of tractors."

It was an effort to bring as much commonness as possible to all products manufactured by Deere & Company facilities around the world. Great strides have been made to achieve this ideal. However, even Deere & Company can't always achieve the ideal. Because the company is global, it has built-in factors that will not yield 100 percent commonality for all products.

Mack commented on this engineering goal. "It's never going to happen 100 percent," he said, "but the objective is to come as close as you can. Sure, there are certain standardizations that can be affected just from a functional point of view. But there's a lot of differences that have to remain. The people in Europe have different climatic condition and cultures. They wanted high transport speeds—tractors that will go 30 miles an hour. One reason is that those guys might drive their tractors into town on Saturday night to see their girl friends."

Draftsmen at work the "old-fashioned way" at the Deere & Company Waterloo, Iowa, facility in 1920. It's entirely possible they are working on blueprints for the Waterloo Boy tractors.

Long-ago drafting tables and T-squares have been replaced by computers at the PEC. Since this 1988 photograph was taken, there have been several succeeding new generations of computers that do the job faster.

Other requirements that are unique to a particular trade area include government regulatory measures. Traffic codes are different, too, which in some instances requires alternative positioning of the lights. The row spacing is different in foreign countries, so there are different requirements in tread width. Foreign governments have different emissions and noise level standards. And it's possible that a government may pass a different set of safety regulation laws down the road. All this brings about requirements that are unique to that particular trade area. All these varied requirements must be considered in the planning stages by the staff at the PEC. But at the same time, the staff is striving for the highest number of possible common features for every market.

PRODUCT TESTING

A vital operation that falls under the PEC umbrella is product testing. Deere & Company tractors and equipment don't go into production until they are tested. Period. The PEC has all the latest test equipment from dynamometers to laboratories, from cold rooms to test tracks, from tilting platforms to farmland. Yes, farmland. Some of this testing

is still done the good old-fashioned way, taking the product to the field and putting it through its paces. The PEC test facilities occupy a 1,000-acre parcel of land where tractors and implements can feel at home in the Iowa dirt.

Much of the testing, however, is machine aided, as machines have the ability to test the tractors or implements at a higher stress rate in a shorter period of time. One such "machine" is the dynamometer. In the test cells, engines are hooked to dynamometers for around-the-clock monitoring of both power output and durability. Afterward the engines are disassembled and examined for signs of excessive wear.

The PEC utilizes a number of different dynamometers, which are essentially just power absorption devices. Applications of the different types include engine, transmission axle, PTO, and drawbar dynamometers. One standard type of dynamometer is essentially a big electric generator. The electricity produced during the test cell operations can be directed into the electrical line and used as electricity in the facility.

In years past, the PEC used dynamometers that pumped water. These types, according to Mack, "were pretty primitive. They were just plain water brakes, nothing more than a fluid coupling. You could control the load by the level of water in the coupling."

Another type of dynamometer is the old type Eddy current for PTO testing. In this dynamometer, a flywheel is heated by the magnetic action between a magnet and big steel flywheel. Because of the heat generated, the unit had to be water-cooled. On the test track, the dynamometers are mounted on carts and towed to test the drawbar pull of a tractor. The cart, or track, dynamometer is also of the Eddy current design, but in this application, it's air-cooled.

Mack mentioned yet another design: "a useful kind of dynamometer was one that our own folks designed. This was just a big multiple-disk brake that was hung on the outside of the axle. It was particularly useful for really low-speed shafts. Essentially, it was a wet clutch running in oil that also served as a heat dissipater or heat exchanger."

A computer, like this one located in the plant at the Harvester Works, can check the progress of a product on the assembly line.

Besides dynamometers, there is also a single tilting test platform at the PEC, which is mounted in the floor. This platform is approximately 20 by 30 feet and hinged on the end. After the tractor is driven onto the platform, it's chained and its wheels are blocked before one side of the platform is raised. If the tractor is positioned to go over backward, it's a longitudinal test. When the tractor is repositioned 90 degrees, the lateral stability of the vehicle can be checked. This tilting also provides information on how the lubricating system and the cooling system will function on severe inclines. These tests are all considered part of the tilting platform activity.

Another means of testing at the PEC is the cold room. This room can plummet the temperature to -30 degrees Fahrenheit to test performance in extremely cold conditions. The hydraulic testing platform examines the impact of stress loads on a vehicle. Loads are mounted on the three-point system and cycled up and down relentlessly hour after hour, day after day, to determine if any part of the system will fail.

Outside the test cells, tractors are hooked to wheeled dynamometers that are towed around test tracks in all types of weather, day and night, simulating various loads to measure power and performance. An outside mud bath tests the effectiveness of seals on wheels and axle bearings. Test units are driven back and forth through the mud bath, hour after hour. Then it's on to the obstacle course, where tractors and implements are relentlessly driven over obstacles far rougher than the product would experience in most farming operations.

According to sales literature, before release, the New Generation model tractors were put through rigorous testing that equaled the equivalent of 10 years of normal use. Regarding these rigors of testing, Mack said, "There was nothing unusual about the amount of testing that was done on the New Generation tractors."

Even though the PEC at Waterloo boasts a state-of-the-art testing facility, no matter how much lab testing is done, there's no substitute for field testing under real-life farming conditions. To provide this final testing, Deere & Company field-tests at its test farm near the Waterloo facility. It also transports tractors and implements to several leased locations around the country. Some years ago, Deere & Company came to an agreement with the King family to test tractors on the King Ranch in Texas. The weather and the enormous acreage available make locations such as this ideal for conducting a lot of test hours on a new tractor.

To ensure that every aspect of a new vehicle is adequately designed, it's subjected to many different tests or test parameters, but the time these vehicles are tested is not equal from test to test. There are hours accumulated in the field, then there are hours accumulated on the test track, then there are hours accumulated on the dynamometer.

These test hours correlate to operational hours. For example, 1 hour on the transmission dynamometer may be equivalent to 3 or 4 hours on the test track or 10 hours or more in the field.

Mack explained, "When you're operating on the dynamometer, you're operating right up to spec load. However, when you're operating in the field, you aren't doing that. For example, when in the field during springtime, you're cultivating at a fraction of the load of which the engine is capable. But when testing on the dynamometer you're up against the peg [engine redline] all the time on horsepower, so over time you establish correlations. For instance, if a pair of final drive gears give up on the dynamometer in a little less than a thousand hours, you might not be too nervous about that. But if they give up in less than a thousand hours in the field, you'd be nervous."

Comparisons are done between the different types of testing to help establish better data. For example, histograms compiled during field testing and dynamometer testing are compared side-by-side to establish correlations and data from which failure modes can be predicted.

Mack continued, "If a vehicle is traction-limited at 4 miles per hour that means that you put on enough ballast to extract full engine horsepower at 4 miles per hour. Now anything faster than that, all the way up to 10 miles per hour, is full engine horsepower. From 4 miles per hour on down, it's drawing less than full engine horsepower because you're traction-limited. In other words, the wheels will spin out. You don't draw full engine horsepower in first gear. And if you do draw full engine horsepower in first gear, you've got way too much ballast on the vehicle.

"So when I say 'redline' or 'up against the peg' this means full engine horsepower down to the traction-limited, or the point at which the wheels begin to lose traction. From there on down the horsepower falls off, although the drawbar pull remains constant. When you run a tractor on a dynamometer, you run it under and in relationship to traction-limited conditions below the traction limit. When you test run it above the traction limit, it's in power-limited condition. Now when you go into the field, it's nowhere near as severe. That's because a lot of the time you're running around empty, pulling wagons, cultivating, and doing things of that nature."

Today, computers have reduced testing considerably because a lot of the failure modes are somewhat predictable. However, the computer can only predict events based on input data available at any one point in the process, so field and lab testing still remain a crucial part of the development process at the PEC.

The new Deere & Company tractors and implements that will find their way to the showrooms and farms of tomorrow are those in the CAD files and on the drawing boards at the PEC today.

CHAPTER 4

THE GENESIS OF GENUINE JOHN DEERE "IRON"

THE WATERLOO FOUNDRY

Tractors and their equipment, which are fashioned from iron ore, originate as products of the very soil and earth that they're designed to till and toil. And the foundry is the genesis of all metal products. It is the initial phase of the manufacturing process and, thus, the beginning of all tractors. There can be no metal products without a foundry. That means no engine blocks, no gears, no crankshaft, no sheet metal, and no tire rims.

The history of the foundry can be traced back to ancient times and threads through the eons up to today. From extracting metal ores from the earth to fashioning the metal into products, tools, and implements, the foundry and its products have evolved along with mankind.

The John Deere Foundry in East Moline, Illinois, had both a cupola foundry and an electric arc foundry. This image shows the electric arc furnace in operation in 1977. The East Moline facility was closed in 1991.

49

Depending on which historical source you embrace, the use of metals in their free state dates back to the Neolithic or New Stone Age of 8000 B.C. An old Hebrew parable from *The Epic of Steel* by Douglas Alan Fisher emphasizes the early importance of iron and the foundry:

When the temple in Jerusalem was completed, Solomon invited to a feast all the artificers who had been engaged in its construction. As the throne was unveiled, the guests were outraged to see that the seat of honor on the king's right had been usurped by the ironworker. Whereupon the people in one voice cried out against him, and the guards rushed forward to cut him down.

The king silenced their protests and turning to the stonecutter said, "Who made the tools with which you carve?"

"The ironworker," was the reply.

To the artificer of gold and silver, Solomon asked, "Who made your instruments?"

"The ironworker," they answered.

To the carpenter, Solomon queried, "Who forged the tools with which you hewed the cedars of Lebanon?"

"The ironworker," was again the answer.

Then Solomon turned to the ironworker, "Thou art all men's father in art. Go, wash the sweat of the forge from thy face and sit at my right hand."

The significance of the foundry was also demonstrated in Rudyard Kipling's *Cold Iron*. It voiced esteem for the role iron played in mankind's developing industrial might:

Gold is for the mistress—silver for the maid,
Copper for the craftsman, cunning at his trade,
"Good!" said the Baron, sitting in his hall,
"But Iron—Cold Iron—is Master of them all."

DEERE & COMPANY FOUNDRY HISTORY

Iron has been central to Deere & Company from the time John Deere lit his first forge to the latest John Deere tractor to roll off the assembly line. Many of its manufacturing centers also included a foundry.

Khalil Kingsbury, retired manager of North American Foundries at Deere & Company, hastened to point out that "yes, they had many foundries. The foundries were a vital part of the factory. And so when

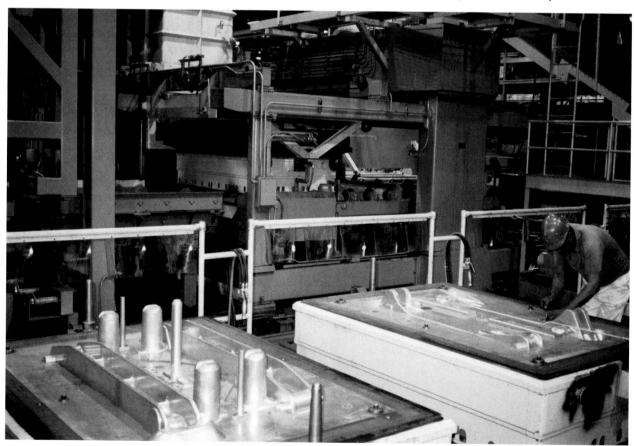

When it was first installed at the John Deere Foundry, this impact molding equipment was the largest of its kind in the United States. Impact molding was a step toward automation in the mold department. It's since been replaced by a totally automated squeeze molding process.

you would think of John Deere Dubuque Works, that also encompassed the foundry. There was a foundry at the John Deere Harvester Works. I think there was a foundry at one time at John Deere Plow & Planter Works. I think you would want to acknowledge that there were a number of these foundries that were all closed over a period of time."

The solitary Deere & Company foundry in operation today is located in Waterloo, Iowa, near the site of the old Waterloo Boy tractor facility. Incidentally a foundry was part of the Waterloo Boy manufacturing plant, which Deere purchased in 1918. While still in operation as a Deere facility, the foundry was referred to as the old M building. The current Waterloo foundry, an electric arc foundry, replaced the old cupola foundry.

The facility is situated on 289.8 acres of land that Deere purchased in 1969. The Cedar River was dredged to provide soil on which to build the foundry and hydraulic building. The plant has 25.4 acres of floor space and a workforce ranging from 400 to 500 employees.

The last Deere foundry to be closed was the East Moline-Silvis Foundry. It was previously a cupola foundry but was upgraded to electric before it was closed. Formerly known as the John Deere Foundry-East Moline, this facility eventually shut its doors and some of its work was integrated into the Waterloo operation.

CUPOLA FOUNDRIES

Prior to the electric-arc operations of the East Moline and Waterloo facilities, the various Deere & Company foundries were all smelting facilities, or cupola foundries, meaning that they weren't a refining operation. They didn't refine ore but rather used pig iron that had been refined from ore at an outside foundry. At a cupola foundry, the metal melt stock was transformed into molten iron, using simply a furnace and stack, or chimney, utilizing coke and hot air to create a high temperature level. Iron and other ingredients were loaded into the furnace. The process would melt the iron down, and it would come out the bottom of the cupola as molten iron.

ELECTRIC ARC FOUNDRIES

Presently, the John Deere Waterloo Foundry is an electric arc foundry. The process is similar to the cupola foundry process because the iron doesn't go through a refining process at the foundry.

The foundry's principal melt stock is scrap metal. Gray or ductile iron are the two main types that are produced at Waterloo. This scrap metal is obtained from dealers who must provide it in a physical size that can be easily handled and loaded into the furnaces. For example, if scrap railroad rails are sent to Deere, the vendor must cut

the rails into specified lengths. In some cases, the metal is reduced by a large shredding machine that cuts metal much like a paper shredder shreds paper.

The metal provided by these vendors and used at the Waterloo Foundry must meet stringent Deere specifications. For example, aluminum isn't ideal for the production of structurally sound iron. Thus, it's imperative that all aluminum be removed from the stock before it arrives at the Deere foundry.

To dispel any misconceptions about a new John Deere tractor as being made from scrap, Kingsbury explained, "There are a couple of things we do. Number one, we have some specific specifications and standards for the scrap iron and scrap steel we use in the melting process. Most of our scrap has traditionally been delivered in railcars, which we'll sample and check.

"We have a process where samples of scrap iron contained in the railcar are randomly acquired in order to make sure the shipment meets specs. And then we have extremely tight metallurgical controls that are checked for compliance all during the melting process. After the scrap is melted, it goes into a holding furnace where it's held before actually [being] used to make a casting. During the melt process and during the holding process, there are continuous metallurgical checks made of the iron to be sure it's within specs before it's poured to produce a casting."

To further ensure casting meets the rigid standard of Deere & Company products, the foundry utilizes Coordinate Measuring Machines (CMM). Castings are randomly pulled and checked on a CMM to validate that the castings are dimensionally accurate.

Commenting on the Waterloo foundry process, retired Deere & Company Foundry employee Bill Bulow said, "We have six arc furnaces. They're capable of melting 12.5 tons of iron per hour and capable of pouring 2,000 tons of iron in a 24-hour period. But we have never actually produced that much. The most good castings poured in a 24-hour period has been 999 tons. Depending on the operation, we run approximately four or five furnaces at any given time and have a standby of one or two furnaces."

Molten iron from the melt furnaces is collected and held in six holding furnaces. It's kept in a molten stage until it's needed to pour castings. Each electric holding furnace can hold 85 tons of iron. How long will iron stay in a molten state in the holding furnaces? According to Bulow, "As long as you want it." The melt department operates 24 hours a day. Each molding unit will run on a staggered shift so it can keep the melt department continuously running. Once the furnaces are started, they're kept operating around the clock.

The electric arc process is deceptively simple: Open up the lid, drop in scrap iron, close the lid, lower the electrodes

Engine blocks and numerous other parts are created at the Waterloo Foundry, which is shown in operation in August 1991. Deere & Company uses updated and environmentally-friendly manufacturing equipment.

above the iron, and then let the arc from the electrodes melt the iron. The electrodes are approximately 8 inches in diameter and 6 feet in length. Electricity drawn when the furnaces are in operation translates to a Deere & Company electric bill in Waterloo, Iowa, of close to $15 million a year, of which $10 million is for the foundry alone.

The Pattern Shop

Before a part can be cast, it must first begin as a part specification. Then it is rendered as a drawing, which in turn is produced as a full-sized molding pattern.

Bulow said, "Years ago, they used to draw it at a drafting table and then send it as a drawing to the pattern shop. The pattern shop would then make a wooden pattern, and then from the wood pattern an experimental casting would be produced. Once the castings were satisfactory, a cast-iron pattern would be made that was used in production. Now all this is done using computers. If a change needs to be made to a part, the changes are first made on the computer. From the computer, the blueprint or computer

drawing can be sent to a pattern company, and the pattern company can make a pattern from the drawing."

For years a pattern shop was an essential part of the foundry process, but the pattern shop has also undergone changes. Kingsbury explains why: "We now purchase a lot of the patterns and core boxes outside, because, again, we could get it done cheaper outside. So the pattern shop, per se, has become a repair shop and a place where we check our patterns and core boxes to make sure that they maintain required dimensional accuracy. It's kind of a quality checking process."

The Melt Process

According to Kingsbury, other operations at the foundry in addition to blueprinting have also been automated. "Although there's an operator in the melt department," he said, "everything about that process is computer-controlled. The holding furnaces are all highly computer-controlled in terms of monitoring chemistry. Then you've got your transfer, your iron pouring processes, that are now computer-automated too. That's a major change from the old manual method where a ladle was moved around on a bridge-crane and muscled into position over a mold and then tilted by hand to pour the iron into the mold. Over a period of years, there's been an elimination of all of the traditional back-breaking jobs through the use of robotics."

The Casting Process

The actual casting process has also evolved—from a labor-intensive "art" of past years to today's highly computerized and automated procedure. Today, as in the past, molds are of the green-sand type. Green-sand or damp-sand molds are formed by mixing sand, clay, or a bonding agent and a small amount of water. A mold is placed into a flask, and the damp molding sand is rammed around the pattern. When the pattern is withdrawn, it leaves a cavity in the sand exactly in the form of the object to be cast.

Molten iron is then poured into the mold and allowed to harden, producing the casting.

Part of the "art" of the casting process was mixing the green sand properly—not too much or too little clay, not too much or too little water. Although there was a formula for the proper mixture, a lot of the success depended on years of experience working with the green sand. A sand mixer would take a handful of green sand and from the "feel" of the sand determine if it was right. The old method required that the sand be shoveled by hand into the flasks and then tamped by hand to the proper compaction density. Too much clay and too much compaction and the gases created by the molten iron couldn't escape from the mold properly. The resulting casting would be inferior. Too little clay and too little compaction and the mold may collapse or deform during the pouring process, producing "sand holes" and an inferior casting. Each green-sand mold can be used only once. Then the sand is

These four-cylinder engine blocks are cast at Deere & Company's Waterloo foundry and will power a multitude of John Deere vehicles, including farm tractors and industrial equipment.

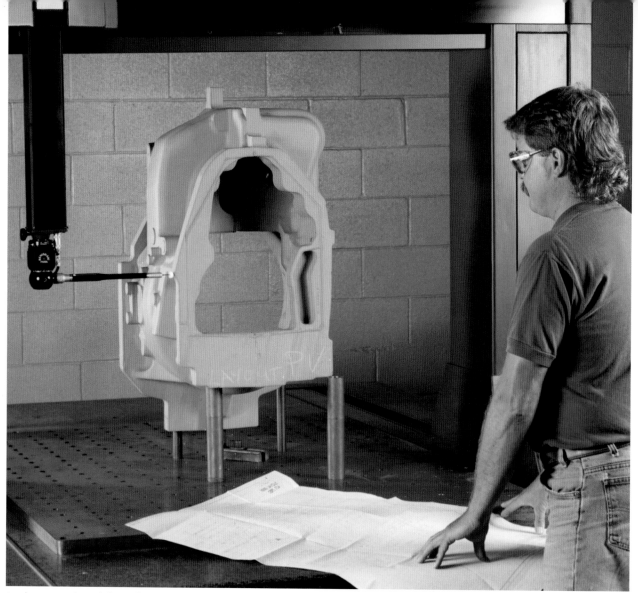

In the metrology lab at the John Deere Waterloo Foundry, a Coordinate Measuring Machine (CMM) checks a foundry casting against specifications to ensure the dimensional accuracy of the product.

used over again in the next mold after the first mold is taken apart. Yes, there was a lot of hand labor involved in this process.

"It's pretty automated," Bulow said of the "art" today. "Now we have sensors to tell when the molding sand needs more water or more clay. A lot of the process is computerized now."

Bulow explains the evolution of the mold-making process: "At one time we used to do it all by hand," he said. "And then they went to what was called a slinger machine to pack the sand into the molds. Then from the slinger machines, we went to impact molds. Impact molding was a process that was used at one time, but it went out with the closure and downsizing of the foundries. It was replaced by squeeze molding. Right now, it's all squeeze molding, utilizing big molding machines where green sand is automatically dropped in the flask and the sand is compressed at 1,500 pounds per square inch. You get an imprint of your mold that way."

Kingsbury also provided some perspective to the molding processes. He said, "We have what we call a computer-controlled automated, high-pressure molding process. It's all automated. The molding units have a pattern shuttle that cycles through a sequence where it's possible to make four, six, or eight different parts at the same time. An indexing table moves a pattern into the molding machine and puts a flask over the pattern, then automatically dump sand into it, which is automatically squeezed. Then the completed mold is moved off onto a mold car, and the indexing table moves the next pattern into the machine with a pattern for a different part. The process will cycle around in a loop and repeat itself."

Small castings can be produced at a rate of 150 to 180 molds an hour. The line producing large castings has an output of approximately 120 molds an hour. Some of the large castings can weigh as much as 1,200 to 1,500 pounds.

Currently, Deere & Company has moved away from producing many of these small castings itself. Kingsbury explains the type of work that the Deere & Company foundry does today: "With the separation of the Waterloo Foundry into its own profit center, we were able to better understand exactly how successful or unsuccessful we were, financially speaking. One of the things that came out of that whole process was that a lot of small castings we had traditionally made, which by the inherent design of the foundries, weren't cost effective.

"A lot of those smaller castings at both foundries were outsourced. It's another way of saying that the Deere & Company factories needing those castings are now purchasing them from outside foundries rather than from the Deere & Company foundry. We were going through a whole rationalization process of trying to understand what kinds of castings we could produce profitably. It was all leading toward larger castings."

Currently, the foundry is casting engine blocks, axle housings, transmission cases, transmission components, pump housing drives, clutch housings, front hubs for the mechanical front-wheel drives, and front-wheel-drive axle housings. This process of determining what can be produced best at the Deere & Company foundry and what is best outsourced is constantly being analyzed and modified as manufacturing and economic conditions change.

Core-Making Process

A not-to-be-forgotten part of the casting process is the core. A core is what's placed in the pattern to form the internal configuration of a casting. For example, take an exhaust manifold. The pattern would form the exterior shape for the casting, and the core would form the interior shape of the manifold.

The core-making process was described by Kingsbury: "Cores are made of sand and resins. The mold-making process could apply to the core room process in terms of the automation that has occurred. The sand is mixed automatically, is put into the machines automatically, and then blown into a core box which is like a pattern that shapes the core. You mix a resin with the sand, and then you inject that mixed sand into a core box, and then you inject it with a gas that hardens the sand."

When the core is finished, it has a shelf life of as long as two years. Once the molten iron is poured into the mold, the heat releases the gas that served as a hardening agent. And the sand is easily removed from the casting when it's finished.

Final Details

After an engine block is removed from the mold, it's cleaned in a blast cabinet by a process similar to sand blasting only using air pressure and steel shot instead. After this initial cleaning, it's sent through a heat treating step that normalizes the casting. It then goes back to the blast cabinet for another cleaning. Finally, it's "chipped and ground" with an air hammer, chisel, and grinder to remove what's called "over iron" occurring during the casting process. Although the Waterloo operation still cleans the castings, the chipping, grinding, finish work, and painting are now outsourced.

EXCEPTIONAL ENVIRONMENTAL STANDARDS

Work Environment

Foundries have often come under attack and suffered from negative public opinions. Foundries have produced a traditional and often accurate reputation of being a dangerous, unhealthy workplace that also has a damaging environment impact. Deere & Company foundries didn't escape this commonly held stigma. Bulow recalled the conditions of the old foundry: "In the middle of winter when you walked into the old "M" foundry, if someone was 15 feet away, you couldn't make out his face because the foundry was so smoky. That was back in the late 1950s or early 1960s. The old foundry was no ideal place to work."

Kingsbury touched on this issue as well: "The foundry is thought of as a dirty place in which to work," he said. "That image was recognized, and I think a tremendous amount of money, effort, and time has been put into the environment of the foundry both internally and externally. The old foundries were dark and dingy and smoky. That's not the case today. They are clean and well-lit."

Emissions

The emissions from the old-style cupola foundries was a significant environmental issue. This was a major reason Deere & Company discontinued the cupola foundries and replaced them with the electric arc melt process. Essentially, the electric furnaces were viewed as being much more environmentally friendly. Tour guides at all of the Deere facilities, including the foundry, commented that one of the most often-heard comments from visitors was about the excellent housekeeping.

Recycling

Although foundries aren't thought of as recyclers, the Waterloo foundry recycles high-grade scrap material. Kingsbury makes an interesting point: "We've always argued that when it comes to recycling, foundries are a proactive part of the recycling process in the United States. We utilize worn-out rail from train systems and worn-out car bodies that are no longer usable. Yet there is a value there, and rather than letting them collect rust in the field they're processed and recycled. We are really a major recycling industry."

FOUNDRY ORGANIZATION AND MANAGEMENT

Management and administration styles and policies have been ever-changing and ever-interesting for a century and a half at Deere & Company. These management changes at the foundries were explained in part by Kingsbury. "The Waterloo Foundry is part of the John Deere Tractor Works today," he said. "Let me elaborate on that for a minute. Before 1986, the Waterloo foundries, and I say foundries because at that time, there was both a cupola foundry and an electric foundry . . . were separated into their own profit centers and became known as John Deere Foundry Waterloo. Prior to that, they'd been a part of the John Deere Waterloo Tractor Works.

"In 1989, the only foundry that existed in Waterloo was the electric foundry. The cupola foundry had been closed. In 1989, we consolidated the John Deere Waterloo Foundry and the John Deere Foundry East Moline under one management structure. Then in 1991, we closed the East Moline Foundry and transferred some of its work to the Waterloo Foundry. Finally, in 1996, we downsized the Waterloo Foundry and reincorporated it back into the John Deere Tractor Works.

"The consolidation of the two foundries under one management structure, in my judgment, was the key to allowing us to make a further critical assessment of the financial viability of the foundries. This led to the decision to close the East Moline Foundry in 1991. I believe the Waterloo Foundry is now shaped or sized so that it's profitable."

OEM PROGRAM

Another changing facet of the foundry is the Original Equipment Manufacturer (OEM) program. Due to the farm economy turmoil of the 1980s, Deere & Company actively sought outside OEM business to keep the foundry running at or near capacity. Deere &

Although not as glamorous as some operations at Deere & Company, it's difficult to build modern equipment without metal castings from a foundry such as this. This 1986 photograph shows work-in-progress at the Waterloo Foundry.

Green-sand molds are prepared for casting at the John Deere Waterloo Foundry during August 1991. By this time the process was moving toward complete automation.

Company concluded that small castings weren't economically viable. Thus, Deere pursued OEM casting business and the casting of larger components and parts. As a result, some of Deere & Company's OEM customers and their products included engine blocks for Pontiac, engine blocks for Detroit Diesel, and drivetrain castings for major customer Caterpillar, Inc.

Kingsbury commented on the foundry's role in OEM business. As the economy changed and the foundry was scrutinized under the profit/loss microscope, Kingsbury said, "I understand a decision has been made to get out of the OEM business. I don't know if that shift has been completed. We were at one point actively involved in the OEM business, though."

THE FUTURE OF THE FOUNDRY

Keeping the foundry profitable and properly positioned within the Deere & Company worldwide organization is constantly changing as indicated by Kingsbury's following remarks: "I believe there's been a decision that in the future all of the cylinder heads and engine blocks are going to be purchased outside. I believe that when we get all done the foundry is going to be really a transmission-oriented foundry. Although the foundry may be producing engine blocks today, I'm quite sure that the Engine Works is going to purchase engine block castings and cylinder head castings overseas. Again, it's just an economic issue."

HOW DEERE PRODUCES THE POWER

THE WATERLOO ENGINE WORKS

I n 1974, Deere's Waterloo, Iowa, engine manufacturing program needed to be either overhauled or scrapped. Key personnel gathered in San Diego, California, for a working retreat to discuss the situation. Their objective was to decide whether the company should continue manufacturing engines at Waterloo or outsource them from another manufacturer.

Retired PEC Director Mike Mack recalls that the retreat brought forward many major disagreements on the Engine Works. The monitor, a professional from outside the Deere & Company organization, proved equal to the task. At the conclusion of the four-day retreat, a decision was reached. Deere & Company would continue manufacturing engines at Waterloo. And the engine program would be expanded to both a new level and a new location. The

This process of installing pistons with the human touch hasn't been replaced by computers or robots.

59

new location would be 139 acres just southwest of Waterloo on Ridgeway Avenue. Construction on the facility began soon after the conclusion of the retreat. Two years later, in 1976, the first engine rolled off the assembly line.

The new John Deere Waterloo Engine Works was, and still is, one of the best engine factories in the world. The factory and office complex is one-third of a mile long, contains 21 acres under its roof, and has the capability to produce 100 different types of engines. To meet production demands, the Engine Works requires some 450 hourly and 400 salaried employees.

INTRODUCTION OF THE NEW GENERATION TRACTOR

Years before the new Engine Works was proposed and built, the old Engine Works had to undergo some major changes. Deere & Company introduced the New Generation tractors in 1960 and the new four- and six-cylinder engines that powered them. The Engine Works then had to completely revamp its tooling to produce multi-cylinder engines in place of the venerable two-cylinder powerplant. At that time, Deere engineers had to establish certain critical dimensions for engine design and corresponding tooling. One such dimension was the center lines for cylinder locations in the block. To Deere & Company engineers, these dimensions are sacred ground.

Only after these dimensions were finalized was the tooling determined and ordered. If the critical cylinder center line is changed, it means that the corresponding expensive tooling has to be changed. The engineering team has to be confident that they have arrived at the right specification because redesigning an engine after this stage isn't a viable option. Not even considering the time required to reorder and install tooling, the price of changing such an engine line today is in the neighborhood of $70 million. Those sacred dimensions, established more than 40 years ago, are still being used on some of the lines at the Engine Works.

Sid Olsen was responsible for the engines and was part of the team that developed the New Generation tractors. Mack commented on Olsen's involvement in the development of these engines. "Sid Olsen really was the father of all the engines that are still built today," he said. "They're a derivative of what Sid Olsen designed back in the early 1950s. They've gone up in displacement; you stroke 'em and bore 'em, but the centerline distance from cylinder to cylinder was what Sid laid out back then. He was a really, really good engine designer."

The Waterloo Engine Works is appropriately situated close to farm acreage on the outskirts of Waterloo, Iowa. In the foreground is part of the test facility where Deere products are put through their paces.

The leaping deer trademark leaves little doubt that this is a Deere & Company facility. In this case, it's the Waterloo Engine Works, Waterloo, Iowa. The plant has the capabilities to produce 100 different types of engines for Deere products and OEM applications.

ENGINE MACHINING AND ASSEMBLY

The Deere & Company foundry in Waterloo provides many of the castings that are used, including cylinder blocks and heads. Some additional castings are being outsourced. Outsourced parts and components are consistently checked with precision tools as they arrive at the docks. The entire shipment is rejected if any part of a shipment is below specifications. Approximately 15 percent of all incoming parts is actually checked to guarantee compliance with specifications.

Cylinder blocks await their turn to begin a journey down the automated machining lines at the Waterloo Engine Works. They could become any one of a hundred different engines that are manufactured at the facility.

This Giddings & Lewis machine performs a variety of operations on either the engine head or block. Some of these functions include drilling and tapping head bolt holes, drilling and tapping main bearing holes, as well as drilling and tapping for the oil pick-up.

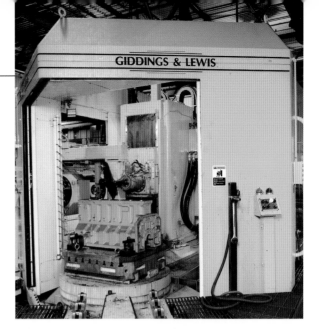

Once the castings pass approval at the Engine Works, the components begin a metamorphosis from rough castings to functional engine.

The initial steps involve the rough machining, such as milling the outer edges of the head or block. After the milling is completed, all drilling, reaming, and tapping operations take place at the next station. After this operation, the block or head is washed and then enters the station where the required finishing work is done. A

This is one of the stations on the automated line at the Engine Works. A cam-in-head unit is getting fitted with its camshaft. This is the engine that replaced the V-8 engine in the large four-wheel-drive tractors.

Here's one of the machining operations that machines a crankshaft from raw casting to finished product. The tolerance on cranks is three microns. A human hair is .0035 inch; a micron is .000039 inch.

diamond hone is used to finish the cylinders, crank, and camshaft. The finishing tool has diamonds embedded in nickel that put a mirror-like finish on the machined surfaces. Next a few internal parts, such as valve inserts, are installed in the head while it's still on the machining line. Then it's washed.

At this point, the automated block line gets a little help from human hands. Main bearing caps are attached to the blocks and marked in preparation for final assembly. Once the caps are installed, bearing caps and blocks are bored out in a line boring process that ensures a precise fit for the bearing.

The engine block then arrives at the assembly line, and the caps are removed. Since they've been marked, they can be reassembled in the correct locations. Another washing is performed followed by an inspection. Then the cam bushing is installed in the block, and it moves to the assembly area.

An employee at the Waterloo Engine Works checks over a "few" crankshafts, any one of which could become part of a John Deere engine that might find its way anywhere in the world.

Racks of pistons with rings and rods are ready to be installed into the proper engines. Pistons are one of the components outsourced from another manufacturer.

Bearing caps are all torqued with a computerized machine that ensures that all bolts receive the proper foot-pounds of torque. This is another example of human workers interfacing with high technology to do the job faster and better.

At the assembly line, every engine gets a birth certificate called an E-form that's attached to the engine as it begins its assembly process. This form is bar coded and carries all the information for that engine. It specifies the number of cylinders, cooling system, engine size, and whether it's turbocharged. This information, coupled with the test results from the actual testing process, gives a history of that engine that can be accessed by technicians in the future if service is required on that particular unit.

The final assembly is done on the J-hook line, which consists of 43 large hooks suspended from an overhead conveyor line. It is 8,000 feet long and winds through the building stopping at 35 stations. The hooks are, as the name implies, shaped like an inverted "J" and are approximately 8 feet high. Each engine block is secured to a J-hook, which suspends the engine at the proper height for workers to assemble components to it at each workstation.

The line is computer-controlled. After the operator puts the block on the J-hook and inputs the type of engine being assembled, the computer program determines the amount of time the engine spends at each

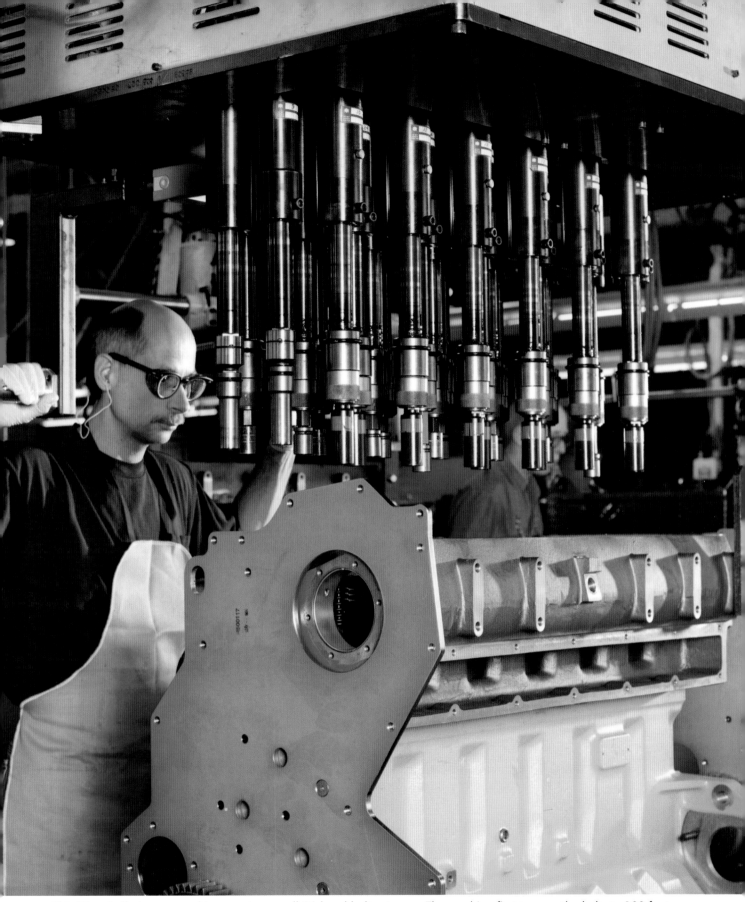

This 26-spindle torque machine can torque all 26 head bolts at once. The machine first torques the bolts to 100 foot-pounds, then backs them off, and once again runs them down to 100 foot-pounds and then backs them off yet again. This allows for stretch of the bolts. The final sequence torques the bolts to 150 foot-pounds.

The J-hook line at the Engine Works moves engines from one assembly station to the next. The line consists of 43 "hooks." It travels 1 1/2 miles through 35 stations.

These are completed engines at the Waterloo Engine Works. Their final destination could be a Deere product or any of several OEM applications, such as other tractors, buses, or even marine ships.

station. Some engines may only call for two minutes between stations, while others may need three or four minutes between each operation. The timing gear gaskets and cover, oil pump, oil pan, flywheel, starters, injection pumps, injection lines, water pump, and damper pulleys are some of the parts that are installed on the line.

Even with the high capital investment of automated tooling, many operations continue to be performed by human hands. Technicians still install pistons into the cylinder block and place head bolts in the proper bolt holes by hand. In the case of the head bolts, as well

A crankshaft undergoes laser testing to ensure that it's within the specification tolerances. The acceptable tolerance is just three microns, or .000117 inch.

An engine block is checked to be sure it meets specifications. These machines at the Waterloo Engine Works are calibrated to 120 millionths of an inch and must be maintained in a strictly controlled environment.

A V-8 engine is moved into one of the test cells at the Waterloo Engine Works. The V-8 engine was manufactured for the large articulated four-wheel-drive vehicles, but it was discontinued in the mid- to late 1980s.

These engines are on the line at Deere & Company's engine manufacturing plant in Saran, France. On May 18, 1998, this facility had the distinction of building the company's 4,000,000th diesel engine.

These unpainted engines at the Waterloo Engine Works are ready to be shipped to the Tractor Assembly facility. All other engines are painted at the Engine Works.

as most bolts, the final torquing is done with computer-controlled systems. This ensures correct and consistent assembly pressure.

TESTING

After the journey down the J-hook line, the complete engine is ready for testing. First, it goes through a leak test for the block, head, fuel lines, and oil lines. Air is pumped at 6 pounds per square inch into the engine. A drop in pressure indicates a crack or cracks in one or more components. Engines that fail a leak-down test are removed from the line to correct the problem and then rechecked until they pass inspection.

At this point the engine is ready to go into the test cells. Test cells have a multitude of high-tech measuring tools to use for scrutinizing engines. The engine is started, run, and subjected to a series of computer-controlled test cycles, which measure performance and detect any problems. The most valuable tool is most likely the dynamometer, which is used to test several facets of engine performance. The engine is accepted if it meets all predetermined performance and durability standards. If there are any aspects that don't meet specified criteria, it is failed and has to be reworked.

The performance of each engine is influenced by the environment in which it operates. Deere & Company engineers, in conjunction with the Society of

This is a view of the J-hook line at the Waterloo Engine Works. Components such as oil pumps, starters, and water pumps are installed on the engine as it travels down the assembly line.

Automotive Engineers, established standards that are maintained to ensure consistent engine performance during testing.

Conditions such as combustion air temperature, humidity, room temperature, and barometric pressure are strictly controlled. If one of these standard conditions change, then the performance may change and compromise the test results. If these factors vary during testing, a complex mathematical formula is used in the test cell computer systems to correct the data to standardized conditions.

Today's precise manufacturing tolerances can't be checked by tape measure or calipers anymore. Checking these tolerances requires special facilities and equipment, such as found in the Deere & Company's Product Evaluation Room, or metrology center, at the Engine Works. This room is environmentally controlled to 68 degrees Fahrenheit, plus or minus 1 degree, is at 50-percent air pressure, and has 20 air changes per hour at a controlled velocity.

All parts to be evaluated are first stored in the room for at least 24 hours to become acclimated to the environment. The computerized Coordinate Measuring Machines (CMM) work with extremely critical tolerances. The parts must be acclimated to these precise meteorological conditions, otherwise an accurate evaluation isn't possible. The table on which the parts are to be evaluated is suspended from underneath by a cushion of air in order to eliminate any vibrations transferring from the building's floor to the table and, thus, affecting the results.

An employee checks engine blocks at the Waterloo Engine Works. Routine checks allow Deere to maintain an incredibly high standard of quality control.

How big is a Micron?
(A proportional comparison)

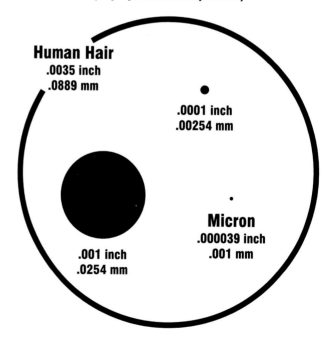

Human Hair
.0035 inch
.0889 mm

.0001 inch
.00254 mm

.001 inch
.0254 mm

Micron
.000039 inch
.001 mm

How close are the tolerances on John Deere engines? This chart illustrates the relative size of a micron compared to a human hair.

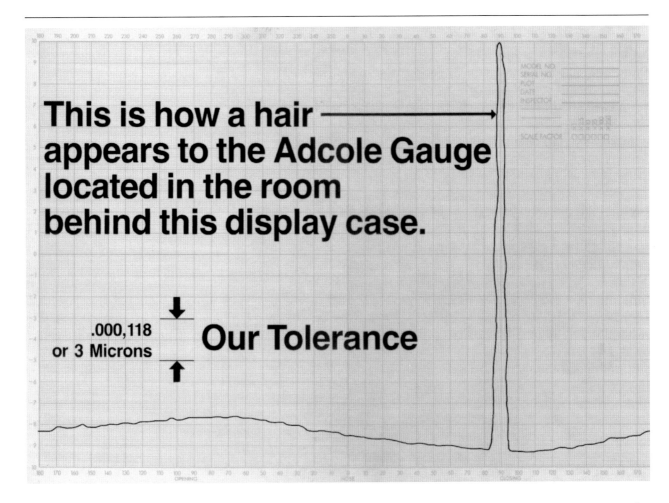

This is how a hair ──────────▶
appears to the Adcole Gauge
located in the room
behind this display case.

.000,118
or 3 Microns ↕ **Our Tolerance**

The original of this graph is displayed at the Waterloo Engine Works, Waterloo, Iowa. As the laser beam scans the crank, it transcribes the data to this graph. To demonstrate the effectiveness of the measuring device, a human hair was placed on a crankshaft and then checked for tolerances. The line on the graph shows that the crank was well within tolerance until it spikes when the hair is encountered.

The measuring gauges are calibrated to tolerances of 120 and 418 millionths of an inch in an area adjacent to the Product Evaluation Room. With such critical tolerances, even airborne particles can pose a potential problem, if allowed to contaminate the precisely machined components. To ensure that airborne contaminates are kept at a minimum, the airflow through the assembly area is pressurized. This directs the flow from the assembly area out to the machining area, and this way any contaminates from the machining operation can't infiltrate the assembly process.

A part to be evaluated, such as engine blocks, outsourced components, or an injection pump, is then placed on the table and the specification loaded to the computer. Then a Direct Computer Controlled (DCC) probe with a needle at the end traces the part and measures every aspect of it. Next, the computer generates a printout, and the results are compared with the design specifications.

OEM PRODUCTS

Engines from Waterloo are found in numerous Original Equipment Manufacturer (OEM) vehicles and products around the world, as well as John Deere tractors, combines, and other farm equipment. Some of the OEM applications include generator sets, marine engines, and stationary engines. Natural gas engines designed and built for installation in Bluebird buses operating in California are an unusual OEM product.

John Deere's engine production capacity is staggering. Diesel engine production began in 1949, but on May 18, 1998, in Suran, France, the company celebrated the building of its 4,000,000th diesel engine. As Ron McDermott, senior vice President, Deere & Company Power Systems Group, points out, "In the past eight years alone, we've produced one million diesel engines, while improving quality in each one."

CHAPTER 6

THE INSIDE LINE ON TRACTOR ASSEMBLY

THE WATERLOO
TRACTOR
OPERATIONS

In 1892, John Froelich built his first tractor in nearby Froelich, Iowa. Only two tractors were built, and both were returned by dissatisfied customers. Despite this, the concept generated enough optimism, and later that same year the Waterloo Gasoline Traction Engine Company was formed in Waterloo. Restructured in 1895 as the Waterloo Gasoline Engine Company, it introduced the Waterloo Boy tractor in 1914. The company was purchased by John Deere in 1918, and it became the foundation for Deere tractor production.

A vehicle is fitted with the appropriate tires and rims. Tires and rims arrive at the assembly station via overhead conveyors. The next tire and rim is visible above the one being installed on the tractor.

THE NEW AND IMPROVED ASSEMBLY PLANT

The original Waterloo Boy factory underwent many expansions and renovations throughout the years to keep pace with the escalating demand for John Deere tractors. Eventually the facility reached its capacity. Meanwhile, projections of future sales indicated there was a need to manufacture more tractors than was physically capable of being built at the original site.

It became obvious that a new manufacturing facility was needed in order for the company to keep pace with anticipated future demands. Deere & Company also wanted to upgrade tooling and manufacturing equipment in its Tractor Works, which would transform the factory into a modern mode of manufacturing.

In 1975, the company moved toward modernizing tractor manufacturing. It purchased land just northeast of Waterloo for the construction of a new tractor factory. Construction of the modern single-story factory began in 1977, and as early as 1979, elements of the tractor assembly operation started. The last portion of equipment transitioned to the new facility in 1981, and it became fully operational.

Since its opening, the Waterloo Tractor Operations has become the crown jewel in Deere & Company's expansion program. The site occupies a total of 1,300 acres, with the buildings and parking lot accounting for 200 acres. The land surrounding the buildings and parking lot has been seeded to native prairie grasses. The new building complex itself has sprawling dimensions that are equally impressive. One thousand three hundred

This 7210 receives the appropriate decals in the final assembly process at the Waterloo Tractor Assembly facility.

An 8400T crawler or track-laying vehicle nears completion on the line at the Waterloo Tractor Assembly plant.

employees work in a complex that encloses 48.2 acres of floor space (or 2,100,000 square feet). (And keep in mind, this is just one of many such plants that Deere & Company operates throughout the world!)

The tractor assembly facility portion alone consists of seven different buildings, only three of which are used strictly for vehicle assembly. Although referred to as different buildings, all seven areas are actually under one roof. The tractor assembly building contains the chassis assembly, chassis painting, and final assembly areas. The second building is the cab assembly, welding, and parts painting building. One building is dedicated to tire and wheel assembly; however, tires are no longer mounted on the rims at the factory. This step in the assembly process has been outsourced. The cast weights are assembled, and everything is made ready for the various options for the different tractors. Deliveries to the line are made via an automated computer-controlled overhead delivery system.

A separate building called the energy center houses air compressors, which provide compressed air to operate tools on the assembly line. In addition, the steam heating system that heats the entire complex is located here.

Although the receiving building still bares the receiving building moniker, it no longer serves that function. This area is now used to build specialty cabs for the 4700 sprayer that's made in the Des Moines, Iowa, plant.

The employee service building includes the lobby and offices for salaried employees, the medical department, payroll, personnel, accounting, and marketing.

Miscellaneous operations prepare tractors for special overseas customers or any vehicles that may require additional work to meet government regulations.

A PROCESS FOR MAXIMUM EFFICIENCY

Right from the initial planning stages, Deere & Company designed the plant to incorporate the best concepts of material flow, process sequencing, and process routing. When the tractor starts its journey down the assembly line, linked computerized work stations ensure that the correct components are installed on each individual vehicle. Each tractor is assembled following a predetermined assembly program, or in Deere & Company terms, a process sequence.

Parts Storage/Delivery

Key to the "process sequence" is the efficient method of parts delivery. To avoid storing parts in bins, parts arrive at the loading docks within hours before they become part of a tractor. Then they arrive at the assembly line work stations as needed. A certain part may be in the plant only for hours instead of the days, weeks, or months that was common with previous manufacturing methods. At the heart of the new system is computerization; advanced computer inventory software programs allow employees to manage inventory routing so that a minimum number of parts and components are required in inventory storage. Not only is

Construction of the Waterloo Tractor Assembly facility began in 1975. This is how the factory appeared in December 1979 when tractor assembly was just beginning. The plant became fully operational in 1981.

this a cost saving, but it also frees floor space for the manufacturing sequence.

Currently, the various components arrive at the assembly point via conveyors, monorails, cranes, or other means, with the assistance of computers. Inside the complex is a 7 1/2-mile computerized overhead crane transportation system used for delivering parts to the assembly line.

Parts Suppliers

An outside supplier may be another Deere & Company factory that builds components for the tractors, such as the Waterloo Engine Works. All the tractors built at the Tractor Works use an engine from Waterloo with the exception of some of the smaller 7000 series tractors. Those engines are built by the Deere & Company plant in Dubuque.

In some cases, Deere & Company uses dual sourcing within the company. There are a lot of major components that have multiple applications on Deere & Company

products. According to Visitors' Services at the Tractor Works, three things are expected of Deere & Company's outside suppliers: meet all specifications, provide the ordered quantity, and deliver on time. Economics plays a large role in the supply scheme too. Outsourcing often proves a sound business move. However, as labor and material costs rise or methods change, this outsourcing trend may reverse itself.

Main frames for the tractors are part and parcel to Deere's outsourcing philosophy. For example, the four-wheel-drive tractor frame is currently being outsourced, but Tractor Operations Manager Donald Duncan indicates that the frame may be manufactured by Deere & Company in the future. (Currently, the frames for row-crop tractors are built in-house.)

The possibility of bringing more of the component construction back to the company is an option. Duncan said, "We can do more in this facility by bringing in some overtime [labor], and perhaps we'll bring a lot of the

This is part of the manufacturing floor at the Waterloo Tractor Assembly plant. The overhead crane system can carry parts around the plant on 7 1/2 miles of overhead tracks.

Painting is one process that technicians still do better than robots, so much better that the robots are now "unemployed" at the Tractor Works.

The Model "D" assembly line at the Waterloo plant in 1924 is a sharp contrast to the present line at the Tractor Assembly facility.

This unit has been fitted with transmission, rear axle, rear hydraulics, engine, and power-assist front axle. It's almost ready for the paint line and a coat of familiar John Deere green.

structural welding back. We really support robotics welding, because it's so repetitive. We never did outsource the cab frames, nor did we ever intend to do that."

While robots can be utilized most effectively when variations are minimized or eliminated, on some jobs robots simply aren't as effective as humans on the assembly line. Duncan adds that, "Our robotics equipment was really getting a little out of the state-of-the-art, and over time we've discovered that to program robots to handle variations is quite difficult. And, of course, every tractor that goes through here exhibits some slight variation.

"On the average tractor, there are approximately 4,500 to 4,700 different parts," Duncan states. And this number reflects only major components such as a carburetor, alternator, or injection pump, and not the number of individual parts within that specific component. Overall approximately 17,000 different parts are on the inventory list to be used in manufacturing all the different models and various options.

Computerized Parts Management System

Helping manage the sheer number and variety of components that go through the Tractor Works is a computer-operated system. Such a system allows the traditional assembly line to coordinate and manage the many components used in assembly. Computers have also revolutionized the information system that's available to the line operator.

When an order is placed for a vehicle, this information, including all options, is entered into the computer. It generates a hard-copy build order, specification sheet, and manufacturing schedule. The documents accompany the unit from inception until it rolls off final assembly line. In addition, all this information is encoded in a bar code tag that also accompanies the unit from start to finish.

Computers are located throughout the plant's assembly area. Enter a serial number into any computer station, and it will immediately locate the vehicle in an area of a few feet. There's a tracer on the side of each unit. As any unit goes by a bar code scanner, the serial number is read and inputted into a computer. As a sort of fail-safe, a computer won't start a vehicle down the line if all the parts, components, and systems aren't available to complete the unit.

A WORLD CLASS PRODUCTION LINE

With the aid of computerized systems, the actual time it takes to produce a tractor has dropped dramatically. Before the introduction of the 7000 tractor, producing a tractor from start to finish required approximately 2 1/2 working days at the plant. Now, even with the increase in options installed, production time has been reduced to just 9 1/2 to 10 1/2 hours.

Although the Tractor Works is two decades old, it is still impressive. How does it measure up to other tractor assembly plants? According to Duncan, "This is probably the newest such facility of its size." As of 1998, the Tractor Works had an 8 to 10 week minimum wait period before a 7000 model was built to order. This lag time would be a little longer on an 8000, with the wait for a 9000 stretching to approximately six months.

Deere & Company has the room and capability to increase production if demands warrant the increase. "We have some room to expand square foot-wise. However, we have a lot of capability to increase capacity because we primarily run a one-shift operation," Duncan comments. "Our capacity constraints aren't this facility, but instead our tier-one suppliers. Components such as transmissions, axles, engines, and a lot of our other outside supply base couldn't easily respond overnight because they tool to a level we forecast."

TRACTOR ASSEMBLY

According to Duncan, the initial step of assembly is when a tractor is "launched." This happens when the transmission is joined to the rear axle. "The serial number on the chassis," Duncan said, "really becomes the serial number for the tractor. There are also independent serial numbers for the transmission, for the engine, for the axles, and for the Sound-Gard body. We build every tractor to a specified order. We have customer orders, we have dealer orders, and occasionally we even have a factory order."

A philosophy that prevailed in 1981 has also changed. Deere & Company formerly would build the product first and then try to sell it. Today the sales are made first and then the vehicle is manufactured.

Tractor assembly itself is divided into three individual areas—chassis assembly area, chassis paint area, and final assembly. The power-operated assembly lines utilize floor conveyers that move the unit from station to station.

This overhead crane moved chassis units into and out of the paint line when the Tractor Assembly opened in 1981. Currently, the units are moved by special forklifts.

For a precise weld time after time, computer-controlled robotic welders weld tractor frames at the assembly facility. Three robotic welding units are employed at the plant. State-of-the-art robotic welding is one contributing factor for John Deere's high standard of manufacturing quality.

The speed of the conveyer controls the number of units eventually coming off the end of the line.

Chassis Assembly

The first stage is in the chassis configuration where the rear axle, rear hydraulics, transmission, side frames, engine, and front axle are joined.

Approximately 30 to 35 percent of the plant's tractors leave the United States for neighboring Canada, South America, Africa, and Europe. It requires 1 to 1 1/2 hours longer to assemble a tractor going overseas than it does a domestic vehicle. Most of the extra time required to prepare these foreign-bound tractors is to meet government regulations.

As an example, two cab doors for the 7000 series are mandated by some overseas governments, while in the United States two doors are an option. On the 8000 series, there's only one door on all models, but some

Tractors cabs are constructed from the ground up at the Waterloo Tractor Assembly facility. Some operations utilize robotic welding, but this particular unit is precision welded by an experienced technician.

foreign governments mandate an additional door. A lever is installed on these tractors that pops out the other side window for an emergency exit. Tractors exported to Germany must have air brakes to adhere to a government regulation. Thus all such units have a compressor installed. Other variations for the German market include lighting systems, fender extensions, a special gear to provide 40-kilometer, or 26-miles-per-hour, speeds, and a special hitch.

Deere & Company offers a wide variety of products, systems, and components for their vehicles. One of the most popular is mechanical assist. It's now ordered on 75 to 80 percent of the 7000 series tractors. Mechanical assist is somewhat similar to four-wheel-drive in a pickup—push a button, and the front wheels are also engaged when more traction is needed. Approximately 90-plus percent of all new 8000 series tractors are delivered with the optional mechanical assist. It's standard on larger tractors.

Chassis Painting Area

When a chassis attains an assembled configuration, it's ready to go through the chassis paint line. Units are moved to the paint booth by a non-computerized

machine—a forklift. From start to finish, it takes about 2 hours and 15 minutes for a chassis unit to go through painting. The steps include cleaning, drying, painting, baking at 190 degrees Fahrenheit, and cooling down in a specific area. A little more than 2 gallons of John Deere enamel is applied to each unit.

When the plant opened in 1981, computer-controlled robots were installed to do the chassis painting operation. From the very beginning, when the system was new, it didn't provide a perfect paint job. Touch-up people were still required to paint what the robots missed. As more and more options and variations were added to the vehicles, it became apparent that the touch-up people were actually doing more painting than the robots. Because a problem or slowdown in the painting process can shut down the entire line, the plant has reverted to using five manual painters to do all the painting of the vehicle chassis.

Electrostatic Depositing Paint System

All other components that go on the vehicle, such as the cab frame, fenders, and wheel rims, are painted by the supplier or in the electrostatic depositing paint system at the Tractor Works. The system paints parts by dipping them into a tank that holds 62,000 gallons of liquid. The paint solution is 90-percent water and 10-percent paint solids. These paint solids are suspended in distilled water, which is charged by 325 volts of electricity. The electrically charged paint particles are attracted to the metal surface, migrating from the water and bonding to the metal surface.

The amount of time and the temperature level control the number of paint particles that adhere to the part's surface. When the proper amount of paint coverage is reached, the component is oven-baked at 340 degrees Fahrenheit, and the paint particles become firmly affixed to the metal. The finished product has an extremely hard, durable surface.

Final Assembly

After exiting the painting process, the vehicle goes to final assembly. The remaining components, such as cab, wheels and tires, fenders, hood, and all the rest of the parts arrive via overhead crane, track, or other means. From this stage, the vehicle is completed with surprising ease and speed. It takes five or six people approximately five to six minutes to install the cab on the chassis. And a

Ergonomics is high priority at Deere & Company. The cab is mounted on rocking-chair-type fixtures which allow the unit to be positioned for maximum convenience of the workers.

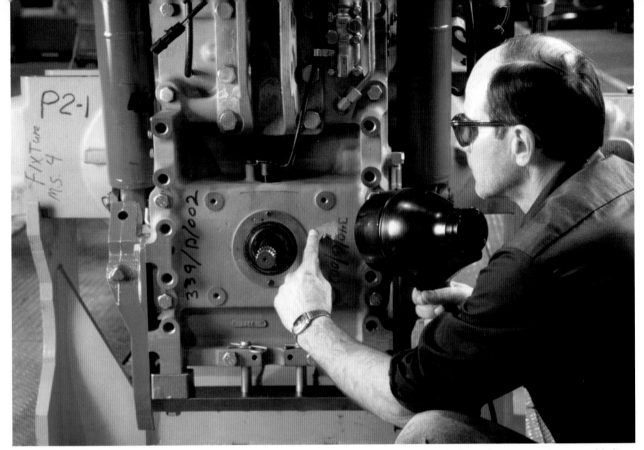

Checking for leaks with a black light is part of the routine testing process that each vehicle undergoes on the assembly line.

A worker utilizes specialized tools to torque down bolts on the assembly line. These specialty tools allow Deere technicians to get the job done quickly and accurately.

skilled assembly line technician requires just 15 to 20 seconds to install each tire and rim unit on the vehicle.

User-friendly tools, which include hand tools for assembly, are standard equipment on the assembly line. Once again, the computer is employed to make the job easier, faster, and more accurate. The computerized torque wrench is one such tool. The specified amount of torque required for a particular task is entered into the computer. A green light on the control unit is displayed to indicate that the proper torque is being applied. A red light indicates a problem and that the correct torque hasn't been applied to the fastener. This indicator ensures bolts are torqued to the proper specification, and it saves a great deal of time compared to running each bolt down by hand and hand-torquing it with a torque wrench.

Many of the tools required for special assembly applications are "homemade," or in other words, they have been made by Deere for the special needs of the line.

Deere's Tractor Works has two notable exceptions to regular assembly line procedure. One is the final assembly of track-laying units. Instead of proceeding through the station where tires are mounted, crawlers are fitted with wheels and driven off the assembly line. Then the units are moved to an area where the tracks are actually hand-assembled onto the vehicle. Two, the larger size and lower production four-wheel-drive tractors are assembled at "stations." Specialized carts are used to move these vehicles to succeeding work stations on the assembly line.

Whether it's a row-crop tractor, a crawler, or a four-wheel-drive vehicle, once the unit is signed off after final inspection, the model number and serial number are entered into the computer. This tells the shipping area that the vehicle is ready to be warehoused or shipped.

Options

The Tractor Works has certain distinct differences from the typical assembly line. Almost every tractor manufactured at Deere & Company's Tractor Works has some differences in its components. Today's tractors have a lot of options, and every tractor is manufactured

An engine and chassis arrive in the assembly station at the correct time, thanks to computer-controlled material flow and process sequencing.

to customer's specifications to give the buyer the equipment needed for a particular job. Options are available on almost every aspect of the vehicle, such as hydraulic equipment, engine, transmission, front axle, mechanical front-wheel drive or regular wide-front axle, front PTO, front hitch, and the number of selectors on the back for hydraulics, not to mention various combinations of tires and wheels. Wheeled tractors have as many as 150 different options just from the axle out, considering wheel weights, tire sizes, tire brands, tread designs, inner weights, outer weights, and axle size.

While there are approximately 200 tractors in various stages of manufacture on the assembly line at any one time, rarely will any two be the same. As an example, Deere & Company builds five different models of its 7010 series: 7210, 7410, 7610, 7710, and 7810. If just one option is changed or varied each day, the company could build a different tractor with a different equipment package daily for more than five years. These kinds of "options" would have brought the old-style line grinding to a standstill. It also would have created an inventory, material flow, and process sequencing nightmare.

UPGRADES AND IMPROVEMENTS

Although the Tractor Works was state-of-the-art when it came on-line in 1981, ongoing upgrades and

Already fitted with the famous Sound-Gard body, this unit is nearly ready for the final assembly process.

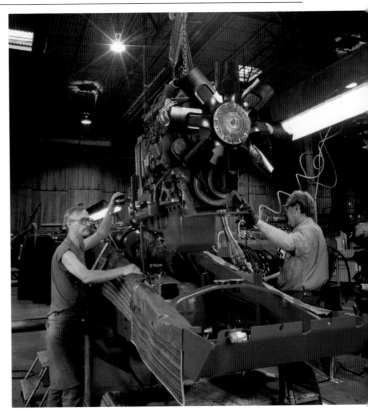

Articulated four-wheel-drive units are assembled on a separate, special line. Here a unit gets fitted with its powerplant.

improvements have kept the facilities at the forefront of the industry.

For example, Deere & Company has completely reversed its philosophy concerning inventory and storage of parts and components. In 1981 when the Tractor Works opened, the name of the game was inventory, and the more you had, the better off you were. To increase capacity, five storage units called high rises were designed and built to manage inventory. Today at the Tractor Works, they're referred to as the dinosaurs, and the only remaining high-rise unit is 300 feet long, 50 feet high, and 50 feet wide. Each of its 7,000 individual storage compartments can hold 2 1/4 tons. At one time such a "dinosaur" stored 500 engines and 500 transmissions. However, the system couldn't keep up with production line demand. When the line was running at capacity, it was always running out of parts.

The storage concept was replaced with a just-in-time inventory concept. The burden for inventory was transferred to the supplier, requiring the supplier to furnish parts as they're needed on the line. The receiving operation was eliminated, and parts are now delivered directly from the truck dock to the assembly line. To further enhance the material flow, the docks for receiving incoming parts were relocated as close as possible to the point in which the parts are used in the assembly process.

THE GOLD KEY PROGRAM

Deere & Company's Gold Key program allows a dealer to schedule his or her customers for a visit to the factory on the day their tractor is being built.

New owners are given a special gold key with which to start their tractors for the first time, a certificate that recognizes them as special Gold Key customers, their name displayed on the TV welcoming them, and a certificate that shows the same TV picture. In addition, they are taken out to both dinner and lunch.

Gold Key customers enjoy a special one-on-one tour with a guide and spend all day observing the building of their tractors. They can actually stand on the assembly line as the tractor moves from one work station to the next. The only part of the operation that they can't "participate" in is the painting process. In addition, customers can ask any questions they want about the tractor, including the test operations. When the tractor is completed, they also have the opportunity to drive it off the assembly line.

Some Gold Key program customers bring their families along so they can visit the Administrative Center and the downtown Pavilion. This is proving a popular program, so much so that in 1998 Visitors' Services hosted around 300 Gold Key customers.

A customer who participates in Deere & Company's Gold Key program receives a gold key like this one for his or her new tractor or combine. The customer can follow production of the machine and eventually starts the vehicle and drives it off the assembly line.

A Gold Key customer and his son watch their combine being built at the Harvester Works in Moline, Illinois.

The same Gold Key program is also available for combine buyer customers at the Harvester Works, and it's proved equally popular. For the 1998 production year, the Harvester Works saw approximately 300 Gold Key program customers as well.

All the Gold Key programs are administered by the Visitors' Services Department, which proudly refers to the program as "Customer service from the heart."

A Gold Key customer receives the gold key for his tractor that he followed through the assembly process at the Waterloo Tractor Assembly in Waterloo, Iowa.

The new system resolved the handling problem and significantly increased efficiency. Before thousands and thousands of parts were unloaded into a receiving area, moved into the old storage system, then retrieved from storage, and finally transferred to the assembly line.

Quality control is improved by having the part inspected immediately as it arrives at the line. If there's a problem with one part, it's just not one part, it may be several hundred or thousand defective parts in storage. To further safeguard quality, any operator has the ability to shut down the entire line, such as when he or she discovers a part that doesn't meet specifications. The suspect part is then routed to an area to be checked by supervisors. Next, the responsible vendor is notified of the problem.

No doubt time and technology will also relegate some existing methods to the dinosaur classification. Regardless, today the Deere & Company Tractor Works is a leading component and tractor manufacturer, employing cutting-edge technology, manufacturing processes, and parts management systems. This has put Deere & Company at the forefront of the worldwide industry.

The shipping and warehousing of completed vehicles are contracted to an outside firm located just across the road from the Tractor Works. This company arranges for shipping by truck or rail, and if the unit is going overseas, by ship to the customer.

THE WORLDWIDE PARTS DISTRIBUTION SYSTEM

Deere & Company has always held a sound business philosophy—take care of the customer. Owners of Deere & Company products rely heavily on the parts and service that the company provides. And it's an indisputable fact that this service is the best in the business.

Indeed, immediate parts availability and prompt, reliable service are responsible for much of the ardent customer loyalty the company enjoys. For a contractor in Alaska, a wheat farmer in Argentina, a lawn owner in the United States, a potato grower in England, or a rice farmer in Japan, prompt and efficient parts and service for products is what keeps them coming back to Deere & Company with their business.

Two distributions centers serve Deere & Company regional depots and dealers throughout the world. The main center is located in Milan, Illinois, while the European Parts Distribution Center is at Bruchsal, Germany. These two main facilities are linked by a

The Parts Distribution Center at Milan, Illinois, covers 1,800,000 square feet of floor space. Each inch of rain that falls on the facility's roof adds 1,000,000 gallons of water to the lake.

computer network that includes 20 regional depots worldwide as well as almost all Deere & Company dealers in 136 countries. This extensive database tracks production, demand, and purchases for more than 275,000 inventoried part numbers.

The Parts Distribution Center (PDC) at Milan and CTI (Customized Transportation, Inc.) located at Plainsville, Indiana, are two central warehouses that serve the worldwide system. The PDC distributes parts classified as slow moving, while CTI serves as the distribution center for high-volume parts and hazardous materials. The PDC at Milan covers a whopping 1,800,000 square feet under roof, and the CTI facility covers 920,000 square feet. Together, they total 2,720,000 square feet—62.44 acres of floor space.

The number of parts shipped is tabulated by individual orders that may be just one part or numerous parts. These are referred to as "lines," and the PDC processes approximately 4,500,000 lines annually. At the CTI operation, the annual lines are approximately 15,800,000 volume parts. Between the two operations, this adds up to 20,300,000 shipments per year.

Of these millions of parts produced and distributed annually, all are delivered to customers with speed, precision, and efficiency. The process starts with 286 salaried and 239 hourly employees at the PDC and 200 warehouse personnel at CTI.

In 1994, a program dubbed RF Storage (Radio Frequency Storage) was launched to improve handling of incoming material and to relocate existing material. Essentially, the project introduced RF equipment and bar code technology to Deere. Today, this program has been evolved to include all aspects of the receiving, storage, and shipping of parts.

Parts need to be identified to fill customer orders and regular stock orders or to provide service. The program

These docks are at the Parts Distribution Center. Every day approximately 35 semi-trailers deliver parts to be inventoried, stored, and then shipped to Deere & Company dealers worldwide.

Deere & Company employees at the Parts Distribution Center are processing FLASH orders. FLASH is an acronym for Fast Locating and Special Handling and is provided 24 hours a day, 7 days a week.

verifies that the correct part is being stored in the correct location. At the point-of-sale, it updates customer and price information on the customer's invoice.

The concept was taken a step further in 1995. Planners from Deere & Company's Facility Planning began working with John Deere Parts Marketing to bring bar code strategies to John Deere dealerships. This program helps provide automatic validation of shipments, and it identifies any discrepancies in an order when a shipment reaches a dealership.

At this time, this program isn't servicing the entire dealer network. In the future, computer and bar code technology will make it even easier to maintain Deere & Company's reputation for excellent aftermarket service. The bar code and computers keep track of the available product and its location.

But before the various parts can be subjected to the bar code system, they must first be delivered and "stocked" at the distribution facilities themselves. At the PDC in Milan, a variety of equipment is on hand to move products. The parts moving fleet consists of 127 forklifts, including specialized High-Rise Lift trucks and Drexels. Plus there's an Automatic Guided Vehicle System (AGVS) to move finished goods from receiving to designated station stops. The system is comprised of 12 vehicles designed with a wire-guided system that allows the vehicles to follow 9,000 feet of wire located in the floor. Each vehicle has a towing capacity of 24,000 pounds and can travel 2 1/4 miles per hour.

The receiving department unloads 30 to 35 semi-trailer trucks a day at 14 receiving docks and processes incoming material from vendors and John Deere North American manufacturing facilities. More than 100 miles

of rack storage provides a home for the incoming inventory. Verifying the quality of products is done by the inspection department. It's helped by on-line access to 500,000 drawings, with another 300,000 drawings available on microfilm. Orders that need immediate attention fall under the customer service's Fast Locating and Special Handling program (FLASH). Customer service provides emergency FLASH service 24 hours a day, 7 days a week.

Other concerns at the PDC include maintenance. Maintenance for the PDC grounds, equipment, and building is handled in-house by the maintenance staff that performs 99 percent of all building maintenance, housekeeping, and grounds care. Nearby is a 4.5-million-gallon lake to provide water for fire protection. Every inch of rain that falls on the building roof provides 1,000,000 gallons of water to the lake. A 33-member fire brigade is completely equipped with its own specially built fire truck and firefighting equipment. Emergency

This is one of the computerized, high-density storage and pick-up systems at the Milan, Illinois, Parts Distribution Center.

The John Deere fleet provides parts and service from the PDC to branches and dealers. The fleet has 48 semi-tractors and 164 trailers that transport 110,000 tons of parts and supplies annually over 1 million miles of roads.

personnel receive extensive in-house training twice a month and at fire school training annually.

The rapid transit of parts from manufacturer to distributor to dealer or end customer is a primary goal of Deere & Company.

Usually, a repair part is an item that's only necessary when it's needed to fix a tractor or piece of equipment which has been in service for some time. Occasionally this sequence is reversed, and parts and service predate the tractor or implements. A case in point is illustrated by the recent sale of 650 John Deere tractors to the Ukraine. By the spring of 1998, 200 units from an order had been shipped.

Don Duncan, manager Waterloo Tractor Operations, commented, "The tractors they have experience with are pretty antiquated compared to the tractors that we're shipping over there. A part of the bid package is service parts. So we ship parts with, and in advance of, the trac-

tors. Part of our product support plan is to have people already in the country when those tractors arrive because there isn't any dealer organization there to support the product. We have a distributor who's set up service shops spaced throughout the country. They have the ability to provide service, and we'll have people with those tractors initially to help get them started right."

The entire Deere & Company aftermarket service is a monumental effort to service customers. It's actually a win-win situation. The customer gets the service he or she wants, has to have, when he or she needs it. And economically, the aftermarket is very good business for Deere & Company. In 1997, its parts sales to North American agricultural dealers topped $1 billion for the first time.

John Deere's pioneering philosophy and Deere & Company's guiding principle have been and continue to be: provide superior products and unbeatable service, and as of 1998, they have been doing just that for 169 years!

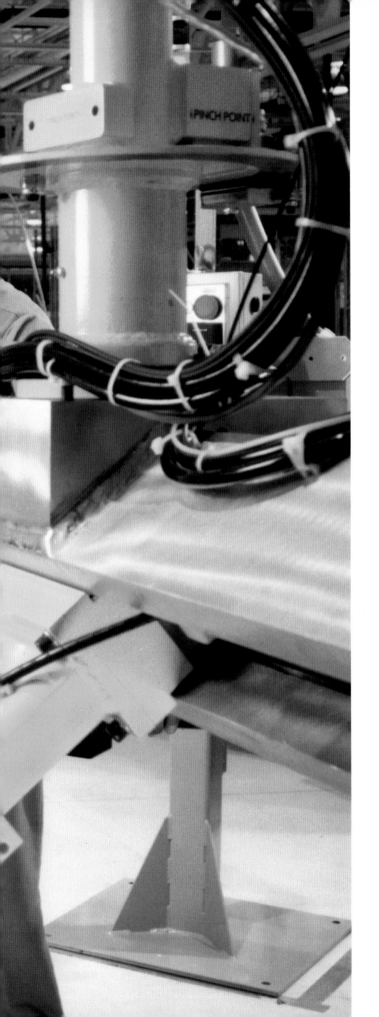

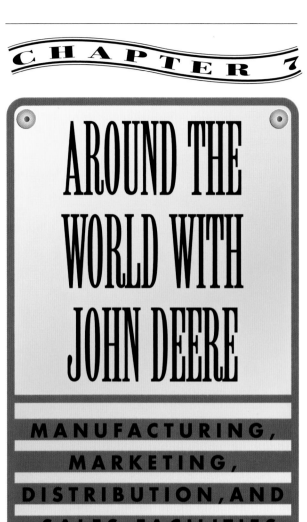

CHAPTER 7

AROUND THE WORLD WITH JOHN DEERE

MANUFACTURING, MARKETING, DISTRIBUTION, AND SALES FACILITIES

O nly a handful of U.S. companies have a history that predates the Civil War. As one can imagine, the history of such companies can become complex and involved over 150 years of growth and expansion. Deere & Company is no exception. Its distinguished and storied history is woven through a civil war, world wars, debilitating depressions, granger capers, union strife, antitrust charges, and yes, the good times too.

The assembly line of Deere & Company's newest engine factory at Torreon, Mexico. This 500,000-square-foot facility produces three-, four-, and six-cylinder engines. On the line when this photograph was taken is the three-cylinder engine for small John Deere tractors.

From the beginning, the Deere partnership and/or corporate name that changed throughout the years was the legal name. But in referring to the company in ads or day-to-day business, the trade or factory names were often used without regard to the actual legal name.

Almost without exception, the branch houses, which were introduced in 1869, used the terms such as John Deere, Deere Manufacturing Company, or John Deere Plow Company in the title of their businesses, even though branch houses were not used in manufacturing. These business entities were separate from Deere & Company although the company could have some degree of ownership. By 1938, Deere & Company managed 100 of these branch stores that were so critical to the Deere marketing network.

Listed below are factory names and dates as they changed over the years. This is not a complete, definitive listing but instead is an overview of Deere & Company, derived from the best information available. Its length magnifies the great amount of history and experience that's connected with the company's growth and success.

John Deere Blacksmith
1829: Leicester, Vermont

John Deere built a small frame structure in which he houses his first blacksmith shop. Within months this facility was destroyed by fire.

John Deere Blacksmith
1830: Leicester, Vermont

John Deere rebuilt the structure and again opened for business. Once again this structure was destroyed by a fire.

John Deere Blacksmith
1833: Hancock, Vermont

After working as a journeyman for a time, John Deere moved to Hancock and built his third blacksmith shop.

Leonard Andrus
1837: Grand Detour, Illinois

John Deere built his fourth blacksmith shop and entered into a partnership with Leonard Andrus. He built his first steel plow.

L. Andrus & Company
L. Andrus Plough Manufactory

This is the entrance to the administrative offices at the Waterloo Tractor Assembly complex. The 2,000,000-plus-square-foot complex produces Deere & Company tractors for a worldwide market. Administrative offices for the Waterloo Foundry and the Waterloo Component Works are also located here.

The Waterloo Boy facility, manufacturer of the Waterloo Boy tractors in Waterloo, Iowa, as it looked in the early 1900s at about the time when Deere & Company purchased the company.

Andrus, Deere & Lathrop
Andrus & Deere
1842: Grand Detour, Illinois

The first formal record of John Deere's partnership with Andrus is March 20, 1843. Most likely, it was a gentleman's agreement before this time. Business was growing, so a new facility was constructed on the Rock River. It was a two-story building with water power to drive the machinery. Luke E. Hemenway was a partner for several months from 1841 to 1842. Horace Paine was brought into the partnership in 1844. On October 20, 1846, Andrus and Deere revised their partnership and included a third partner, Oramil C. Lathrop. Apparently, Paine left the partnership. Lathrop left the partnership on June 22, 1847.

Deere & Tate
John Deere Plow Works
Moline Plow Factory
1848: Moline, Illinois

John Deere dissolved his partnership with Leonard Andrus in May 1848 and relocated on the Mississippi River at Moline. Deere and an employee from Grand Detour, Robert N. Tate, signed a formal partnership on June 19, 1848. A new building that had 1,440 square feet of floor space was constructed. John M. Gould entered the partnership in the fall of 1848.

Deere, Tate & Gould
Deere, Atkinson & Company
John Deere
Deere & Company
Moline Plow Works
John Deere Plow Works
1849: Moline, Illinois

A new structure of 4,800 square feet was added, making a total of 6,240 square feet at the facility. Deere, Atkinson & Company never became a formal partnership, and Charles Atkinson remained with the business only a short time. The Deere, Tate & Gould partnership disbanded in 1852, with Deere buying out Tate & Gould.

"John Deere" began operation. Letterheads and advertisements also refer to the name "Moline Plow Manufactory" during the period after Deere becomes the sole proprietor. Also as his son-in-law James Chapman becomes involved in the business, there was some references to the business as Deere & Chapman. However, records don't confirm that this was ever a legal entity.

On July 1, 1857, the firm was legally organized as Deere & Company with four partners: John Deere, Charles Deere, Luke Hemenway, and David H. Bugbee. On March 13, 1858, Deere & Company was dissolved with ownership reverting to John Deere. By October 5, 1858, the elder Deere deeded all his interests in the firm to his son, Charles Deere.

In December 1858, Charles Deere brought his brother-in-law Christopher Webber into the partnership.

Webber left the partnership by 1860. In 1864, Deere & Company became the legal name of the company again.

The business was first incorporated as Deere & Company on August 15, 1868. The abbreviated form, Deere & Co., was often used, but it wasn't a legal name of either a partnership or a corporation.

In 1870, the Plow Works buildings totaled 90,000 square feet. By 1882, building space covered 9 acres, and electric lights were installed. Floor space grew to 35

These John Deere Model D tractors with dual rear wheels and rubber tires make an impressive lineup in front of the Waterloo Tractor Company in 1931.

In the early 1940s, the Waterloo plant was a contractor for the fabrication and production of transmissions and final-drive units for the U.S. Army's M3 tank. Transmission gears are being cut on the machines pictured here.

JOHN DEERE PLOW WORKS
LARGEST STEEL PLOW FACTORY IN THE WORLD

This turn-of-the-century photograph bills the Plow Works at Moline, Illinois, as the largest steel plow factory in the world. Stacks of lumber are located on the far left and far right. At about this time, Deere was using 2,000,000 feet of hardwood lumber a year in its products.

The John Deere Harvester Works in East Moline, Illinois, resides on the site of the old Root and Vandervoort plant, that produced Deere's first binders.

acres by 1904. By 1911, 20 miles of overhead trolley tracks were in use to move products.

In 1966, the Plow Works had grown to 1,730,163 square feet. In January 1969, John Deere Industrial Equipment Works was established as a division of John Deere Dubuque Tractor Works. It was consolidated with John Deere Plow Works and John Deere Planter Works into one operating unit known as John Deere Plow & Planter Works on June 22, 1971.

In June 1986, the Plow & Planter Works was consolidated as part of the Harvester Works management structure. During the late 1980s, most of the old facility was torn down and the land deeded to the City of Moline for construction of a new Civic Center.

At that time, the plow production was outsourced, and for the first time since John Deere made his first plow, Deere & Company wasn't producing a plow.

Currently, plows are still manufactured for the Mexican market in Monterrey, Mexico.

Moline Wagon Company
John Deere Wagon Company
John Deere Wagon Works
1850: Moline, Illinois

James First began making farm wagons in Moline, Illinois, just three years after John Deere moved his business from Grand Detour. The enterprise was incorporated in 1872 as the Moline Wagon Company. Eventually, annual production reaches 30,000 wagons, making it one of the largest wagon manufacturers in the world.

In about 1880, Deere & Company began to sell these wagons through its branch houses and subsequently purchased the business in 1911. Part of this facility later became the Moline Tractor Works.

This aerial view illustrates the East Moline, Illinois, facility that was renamed the Harvester Works in 1974. If you look closely, you can see lines of red in the corner. That is one of the "other" implement companies located next door to Deere & Company.

This is East Moline's Union Malleable Iron Company as it appeared in 1898. It became part of Deere & Company in 1911.

The name was changed to John Deere Industrial Equipment Works on December 1, 1958. John Deere Industrial Equipment Works was established as a division of John Deere Dubuque Tractor Works in January 1969. It consolidated with John Deere Plow Works and John Deere Planter Works into one operating unit known as John Deere Plow & Planter Works on June 22, 1971.

Today, this facility produces hydraulic cylinders for Deere agricultural and construction equipment, as well as a number of OEM customers.

Marseilles Manufacturing Company
John Deere Spreader Works
1859: Marseilles, Illinois

Augustus Adams invented a force-fed automatic corn sheller. He also designed and manufactured one of the first successful grain elevators. He and his sons began manufacturing these items at Marseilles in the mid-1890s.

In 1908, Deere & Company purchased the business. This business and the Kemp & Burpee Manufacturing Company became part of the John Deere Spreader Works on December 31, 1916, at an East Moline location.

In 1965, the Spreader Works plant had 791,132 square feet of floor space. It was combined with John Deere Harvester Works to become John Deere East Moline Works on April 18, 1969. This building later became part of John Deere Parts Company and then the Parts Distribution Center (PDC).

Van Brunt Manufacturing Company
John Deere Horicon Works
1860: Mayville, Wisconsin

The Van Brunt Manufacturing Company was founded by Daniel and George Van Brunt. They moved to Horicon, Wisconsin, in 1862. The Van Brunt Manufacturing Company became part of Deere & Company on June 24, 1911. The Van Brunt operation produced grain drills in Horicon until the mid-1960s. At that time, grain drill production was moved to the Des Moines works. By 1965, this facility had grown to 632,090 square feet.

In 1963, Deere & Company introduced its first lawn and garden tractor, which was produced at Horicon. The lawn and garden product offering increased to include all manner of garden equipment (walk-behind mowers, tillers, snowblowers, and attachments).

The product line evolved into the Consumer Product Division and included snowmobiles, bicycles, and other types of equipment at various times. Eventually, this factory became the Lawn and Grounds Care Division and eventually the Consumer and Commercial Equipment Division in 1996.

In 1976, a second manufacturing facility was added to the original Horicon plant. The marketing and certain administrative functions moved from Horicon to Raleigh, North Carolina, in the early 1990s. Today,

Horicon produces lawn tractors, riding lawn mowers, and attachments for these products.

Union Malleable Iron Company
John Deere Malleable Works
1872: Moline, Illinois

Union Malleable Iron Company was founded expressly for the purpose of providing malleable castings, pearlitic castings, and white-iron castings to almost all of the John Deere factories. Charles Deere, at the time vice president of Deere & Company, helped organize the new company. Deere purchased the company on April 7, 1911.

Operations were consolidated into John Deere Foundry in 1968.

A customer picks up a new John Deere 9610 Maximizer combine at the East Moline Harvester Works.

This is the combine assembly line at the Harvester Works in Moline, Illinois, in March 1998. Whether building tractors or combines, the actual "line" functions quite similarly.

A John Deere combine is put through computerized testing at the Harvester Works. The "big" John Deere 55 model was considered a big combine. However, the CTS II Maximizer redefines "big" combine.

Syracuse Chilled Plow Company
1876: Syracuse, New York

The Robinson Chilled Plow Company was reorganized in 1879 as the Syracuse Chilled Plow Company. Founder Thomas Wiard obtained a patent for compounding and chilling cast iron to render it more suitable for plow shares. Deere & Company purchased the company in 1911. The decision to discontinue operations at the factory was announced October 20, 1952.

Deere & Mansur Company
Deere & Mansur Works
1877: Moline, Illinois

The Deere & Mansur Works was another company that Charles Deere helped establish to provide a needed product for the Deere & Company line. The company's planters became an important step in providing Deere with a full line of implements to market through its branch houses.

Even though Charles Deere was the company's first president, it didn't become a Deere company until 1911 when Deere & Company purchased it.

In 1971, the Planter Works, John Deere Plow Works, and John Deere Industrial Equipment Works were merged into the John Deere Plow & Planter Works.

Kemp & Burpee Manufacturing Company
1877: Magog, Quebec

The Kemp & Burpee Manufacturing Company was moved to Syracuse, New York in 1880. It built and

This is the entrance to the Dubuque, Iowa, office complex. In 1945, Deere & Company purchased property for a new plant in which to build the Model M tractor. Its history includes production of two-cylinder tractors, engines, New Generation model tractors, and construction equipment.

marketed the first practical manure spreader. In 1911, Deere & Company purchased Kemp & Burpee Manufacturing Company and began production of the manure spreader at the Marseilles plant in East Moline, Illinois.

Dain Manufacturing Company
John Deere Ottumwa Works
1881: Meadville, Missouri

Joseph Dain founded this company that pioneered hay handling equipment. The sweep rake and hay stacker were the company's first implements. The company moved to Springfield, Missouri, then to Armourdale, Kansas, and then to Carrolltown, Missouri, where it was incorporated in 1890.

In 1900, the company moved to Ottumwa, Iowa. Subsequently, it added stationary and automatic windrow pick-up presses, hay choppers, field ensilage harvesters and blowers, and pump jacks. Dain Manufacturing Company was acquired by Deere & Company on November 1, 1910.

By 1965, the facility covered 1,015,791 square feet of floor space.

1886: John Deere died.

Reliance Buggy Company
1891: St. Louis, Missouri

This company's yearly capacity was 20,000 vehicles and was an important part of Deere & Company until the automobile became popular. It was one of the factories acquired during the 1911 mergers.

Killefer Manufacturing Corp. Ltd.
John Deere Killefer Works
1892: Los Angeles, California

Killefer Manufacturing Corp. Ltd. manufactured a line of heavy agricultural equipment. The company was purchased by Deere & Company on July 1, 1937, and operated as the John Deere Killefer Works. In 1965, the plant covered 256,630 square feet. The facility was closed January 6, 1969.

Waterloo Gasoline Traction Engine Company
Waterloo Gasoline Engine Company
1893: Waterloo, Iowa

The Waterloo Gasoline Engine Company was founded by John Froelich with the idea of powering a steam traction engine with a gasoline engine. It was one of the first successful "tractors."

A 1977 aerial view illustrates the Davenport Works, Davenport, Iowa. Originally the Davenport Wagon Company, founded in 1904, the facility was purchased by Deere & Company in 1911.

Here's the G-Series dozer line at Deere & Company's Dubuque, Iowa, plant. This facility is a main producer of Deere's construction equipment line.

The company was purchased by Deere & Company in 1918, and the tractors retained the Waterloo Boy name until the John Deere Model D was introduced in 1923. The word "gasoline" in the company name was misleading as its early two-cylinder tractor engines actually burned kerosene.

A name sometimes associated with the Waterloo plant was the Iowa Transmission Company. This separate Deere & Company division manufactured transmissions and final-drive units for the M3 tank during World War II.

By 1965, a total of 3,774,405 square feet of floor space was under one roof.

Fort Smith Wagon Company
1903: Fort Smith, Arkansas

The Fort Smith Wagon Company was a successor to the South Bend Wagon Company. The Fort Smith concern was located in excellent hardwood country and made an equally excellent product. Deere & Company branch houses began offering these wagons in 1905. Deere & Company purchased the concern on April 24, 1907. In 1925, all land and buildings of the company were sold, and the wagon business transferred to Deere Wagon Works of Moline.

Davenport Wagon Company
1904: Davenport, Iowa

In 1908, new facilities were constructed to begin manufacture of a steel wagon. Deere & Company purchased the business in 1911.

This overhead aerial view of the Des Moines, Iowa, plant was taken in 1979. There is more than 2,000,000 square feet of floor space at this Deere & Company facility, where cotton harvesting, tillage, planting, and spraying equipment is produced.

Des Moines Ordnance Plant at Ankeny, Iowa, in 1948, one year after Deere & Company purchased the facility. Corn pickers were one of the first items moved to the plant for production.

1907: Charles Deere died.

Dain Manufacturing Company, Ltd.
1908: Welland, Ontario, Canada

This was a small subsidiary that Dain opened before the parent company was bought by Deere & Company. It was included in the sale to Deere. Harvesters were produced on an experimental basis, aimed at the Canadian trade, with several being tested in 1910.

It merged with John Deere Plow Company of Welland, Ltd. on October 21, 1918, to become John Deere Manufacturing Company, Ltd. The manufacturing operations were mothballed in 1923 but resumed again in 1931.

The John Deere Manufacturing Company, Ltd. corporation was discontinued September 8, 1937. Assets went to John Deere Plow Company (Ltd.), which became John Deere Welland Works on October 15, 1935.

Growth expanded the facility to 708,981 square feet of floor space by 1965.

John Deere Export Company
1911: New York, New York

John Deere Export Company was established as a separate Deere & Company organization for exporting its own products and also equipment of other manufacturers.

Deere & Company
1911: Moline, Illinois

A new holding company was put into place for the proposed reorganization and acquisition program set forth by the company directors. It was the same name as previously incorporated.

John Deere Spreader Works
John Deere East Moline Works
John Deere Harvester Works
1911: East Moline, Illinois

The John Deere Harvester Works was founded in rented quarters at the old Root & Vandervoort plant. During the winter and spring of 1912, 2,000 harvesters—binders—were produced. A circus tent was erected on the property to provide extra space for assembly and storage.

The initial Deere & Company–owned Harvester plant was constructed in 1912. In 1913, corn binders were added to production. In 1914, mowers and sulky rakes were placed into production.

In 1944, at the behest of the War Production Board, part of the corn picker production was transferred from John Deere Harvester Works, East Moline, Illinois, to Minneapolis,

Minnesota. Some of the production was performed at the Deere & Webber Company warehouse. This company was a Division of Deere & Webber Company known as The Corn Picker Assembly Plant of Deere & Webber Company. In 1946, production stopped at the Minneapolis plant and was transferred back to the John Deere Harvester Works.

In 1969, the John Deere Spreader Works and the John Deere Harvester Works were consolidated into one manufacturing unit. The resulting complex was named the John Deere East Moline Works. On May 1, 1974, the John Deere East Moline Works was renamed the John Deere Harvester Works.

As of 1965, this plant covered 2,832,465 square feet or 65 acres.

Vermilion Malleable Iron Works
John Deere Vermilion Works
1912: Hoopeston, Illinois

The Vermilion Malleable Iron Works was a foundry producing malleable castings. Initially owned by Poor & Company, it was purchased by Deere & Company on

In 1942, Security personnel stand watch at the John Deere Spreader Works, and no, they weren't guarding manure spreaders. Deere's contribution to the war effort required security at the facility.

WHERE THE *GREAT DAIN LINE* OF HAY TOOLS ARE MADE
DAIN MANUFACTURING CO.
OTTUMWA, IOWA

Deere & Company acquired the Dain Manufacturing Company in 1910. This plant in Ottumwa, Iowa, manufactured haying equipment. The Dain name was one of the few trademark names to remain on a product after Deere's purchase.

April 1, 1946. Known as the Vermilion Malleable Iron Works, it provided malleable iron castings for John Deere factories for 31 years. It was sold to the Vermilion Iron Corporation in 1977.

Moline Timber Company
1913: Portland, Maine

This corporation was dissolved on July 15, 1935.

Lindeman Manufacturing, Inc.
John Deere–Lindeman Works
John Deere Yakima Works
1923: Yakima, Washington

In 1940, Deere began supplying Lindeman Manufacturing Company with Model BO tractor chassis to which Lindeman fits its own crawler tracks. Deere bought the Lindeman company in 1945. The Yakima facility continued to manufacture the tracks that were shipped to Dubuque where the tractors were manufactured. The Yakima plant was closed in 1953, and track production moved to Dubuque.

In 1949, the name was changed to John Deere Yakima Works. The John Deere–Lindeman Company was formally dissolved in 1950. In 1953, the John Deere Yakima Works was closed.

Funk Manufacturing, Inc.
1936: Akron, Ohio

Akron Aircraft Company was founded in Akron, Ohio, by the Funk twins, Joe and Howard. The company later moved to Coffeyville, Kansas, and the company was renamed the Funk Aircraft Company. In 1946, plane production was discontinued and switched to other products, including tractor transmissions and stationary power plants. Deere & Company purchased the company in 1989.

John Deere Dubuque Tractor Company
1945: Dubuque, Iowa

Land was purchased for new factory construction to build the Model M tractor. Production began in mid-1947.

The Moline Tractor Works was transferred to Dubuque in 1946. At this time, the Moline Tractor Works facilities became part of the John Deere Wagon Works in order to provide more factory space for implement production.

The Dubuque factory became the home of Deere & Company's Industrial Equipment Division and was renamed the Construction Equipment Division in 1996. A variety of products were produced in Dubuque, including bulldozers, self-propelled scrapers, motor graders, front loaders, skidders, and backhoe loaders.

With the construction of the Davenport Works, Davenport, Iowa, front loaders, skidders, and motor graders were moved to Davenport. Self-propelled scrapers were outsourced in the 1980s, and currently, Dubuque produces bulldozers and backhoe loaders. The product engineering function for construction equipment is also housed at Dubuque.

By 1966, this production facility grew to 2,031,386 square feet.

John Deere Des Moines Works
1947: Des Moines, Iowa

Deere & Company purchased the Des Moines Ordnance Plant at Ankeny, Iowa. The facility included five large industrial buildings, a power plant, a sewage disposal plant, and various smaller structures, including approximately 400 acres of land.

Initially, certain implements produced at the John Deere Plow Works were to be transferred to the Ankeny plant. That included the entire line of corn pickers. In 1949, manufacture of all John Deere row-crop cultivators was also transferred to this plant. Floor space under roof reached 2,212,401 square feet by 1965.

Combine corn heads were produced here for a period until this production was moved to the Harvester Works.

Cotton pickers were by far the key product line for Des Moines. Cotton picker production began in the late 1960s. Self-propelled sprayers were introduced into production to complement the product offering to cotton farmers. However, the sprayer production was

This factory in Welland, Ontario, was part of Dain Manufacturing Company, which Deere purchased in 1910. Interestingly enough, railroad tracks, railroad cars, and horse and wagon are on the factory roof.

John Deere hay and forage equipment is manufactured at this Deere & Company plant in Ottumwa, Iowa. Today's John Deere Ottumwa Works was originally the Dain Manufacturing Company.

moved to Louisiana in 1995. Currently, the Des Moines factory produced tillage equipment, grain drills, and cotton harvesting equipment.

Grand River Chemical Division of Deere & Company
John Deere Chemical Company
1951: Pryor, Oklahoma

Deere & Company made the decision to enter the fertilizer industry. A plant was constructed at Pryor, Oklahoma, and called the Grand River Chemical Division of Deere & Company. Production began in 1954. In 1960, the name was changed to the John Deere Chemical Company with added facilities at Tulsa, Oklahoma. In 1965, the chemical company was sold to Nipac, Inc. of Dallas, Texas.

Deere & Company
1958: Merger

A company bulletin dated July 30, 1958, notified that a change of names occurred on August 1, 1958.

Deere & Company, Deere Manufacturing Company, John Deere Van Brunt Company, and John Deere Killefer Company was merged into a new corporation named "Deere & Company." This effectively made all manufacturing plants in the United States part of and owned by the corporation "Deere & Company."

Deere & Company Administrative Center
1964: Moline, Illinois

New Deere Administrative Center opened. An addition to the Administrative Center was opened in 1977. This addition nearly doubled the amount of office space. It continued the distinctive exterior design. An atrium was a unique feature in the center of the facility.

John Deere Foundry
1966: East Moline-Silvis, Illinois

Construction of a new foundry, which was known as the Foundry Unit, began. Foundry Unit construction was completed on November 1, 1968. The official name as of

A 1977 aerial view illustrates the Davenport Works at Davenport, Iowa. Today, this Deere & Company plant manufactures construction and forestry equipment.

June 19, 1968, was John Deere Foundry. This facility was closed in 1991 and stood idle until its sale in 1997.

1972: Waterloo, Iowa

A new electric foundry was built on a downtown Waterloo site. It poured its first iron in September. This all-electric foundry had a capacity of 200,000 tons of gray iron.

John Deere Davenport Works
1973: Davenport, Iowa

Construction began in 1973. It was a facility for manufacturing construction and forestry equipment.

John Deere Waterloo Engine Works
1976: Waterloo, Iowa

Deere's new state-of-the-art engine facility began producing engines for John Deere products and OEM customers. It was the administrative center for Deere's Power Systems Group (DPSG).

John Deere Waterloo Tractor Operations
1981: Waterloo, Iowa

New Tractor Works was completed and began operation. It produced large row-crop tractors for the worldwide market. The downtown facility, renamed the Component Works, produced axles, transmissions, and

This is a 1981 image of the John Deere Davenport Works motor grader assembly line.

hydraulic components. It also specialized in machined parts for Tractor Works, Engine Works, and Industrial Equipment Division products produced in Dubuque and Davenport.

In 1990, the Tractor Works and the Component Works were recombined into one administrative organization. After 1990, several of the older buildings in the downtown facility were razed.

John Deere Rotary Engine Division
1984: Wood-Ridge, New Jersey

Initially the rotary engine experimental program was viewed as a possible alternative power source for farm equipment. At least one Model 2950 tractor was fitted with a rotary engine for test purposes. It didn't measure up to environmental or fuel efficiency standards,

and the Rotary Engine Division was sold in 1990.

John Deere Power Products, Inc.
1989: Greeneville, Tennessee

In 1989, the factory opened to produce walk-behind mowers. Before this, walk-behind mowers were produced in Horicon.

John Deere Commercial Products
1991: Augusta, Georgia

The Augusta factory was built to produce a small compact utility, and utility tractor for commercial applications. The 4000 line of 20–30 horsepower tractors was relocated from the Horicon factory. The 5000 line of 40–60 horsepower tractors was initiated in 1992. The factory is an assembly-only facility.

1994: Moline, Illinois

The old "Bolt Room" that had made plow bolts and John Deere hardware for many years was closed. The John Deere Pavilion was opened on that same site.

1995: Moline, Illinois

The planter production facility was renamed the Seeding Division, and its management structure was separated from the Harvester Works. The remnants of the old Industrial Equipment Division, which now produces hydraulic cylinders, became known as the Cylinder Division. It still administratively reports to the Harvester Works.

John Deere Handheld Products Division
1994: Columbia, Gastonia, and Greer, South Carolina

These factories in South Carolina are part of the former Homelite Company that Deere acquired from Textron.

John Deere Turf Care
1995: Raleigh, North Carolina

This factory produces a variety of golf and turf care equipment. Greens mowers and fairway mowers are part of the product line.

John Deere Worksite Products
1998: Knoxville Tennessee

It manufactures Deere & Company's proprietary line of skid steer loaders. Skid steer loaders had been produced for Deere by New Holland.

OVERSEAS

Heinrich Lanz
John Deere–LANZ A.G.
1859: Mannheim and Zweibrucken, Germany

Founder Heinrich Lanz, originally an importer of agricultural machinery, built his own line of agricultural machinery around 1869. In the 1870s, his company moved into manufacture of stationary steam engines.

In June 1967, John Deere-Lanz was sold to Deere & Company, but it had been a wholly owned subsidiary. Marketing and manufacturing were one entity from 1956 to 1963.

In 1956, its factories covered 2,500,000 square feet and employed 8,000 people.

Combine production was moved from Mannheim to Zweibrucken in 1963. In 1964, John Deere Zweibrucken was created as a separate factory from Mannheim.

The four-wheel-drive loader assembly line at John Deere Davenport Works in 1981.

The Van Brunt Manufacturing Company at Horicon, Wisconsin, had been renamed the John Deere Horicon Works by the time this aerial photograph was taken in 1979. The street blocks provide a sense of the plant's scale.

Founded in 1860, the Van Brunt Manufacturing Company was purchased by Deere & Company in 1911. The company's line of grain drills helped Deere become a full-line supplier. This shows the facility in Horicon, Wisconsin, as it was in 1941.

John Deere Argentina
1958: Rosario, Argentina

Deere & Company constructed a new plant to build a maximum capacity of 3,000 agricultural tractors per year. A separate sales branch was established in Buenos Aires. In 1978, the sales branch and the factory were consolidated into one entity located at Rosario. Although tractor production continued through 1995, it was at an extremely low level.

In 1996, the engine manufacturing was upgraded as part of a larger "Mercosul" project. Rear axles and non-powered front-axle production were also upgraded. Tractor production was transferred to SLC-John Deere in Brazil.

Compagnie Continentale de Motoculture (CCM)
Compagnie Française John Deere
1959: Arc-les-Gray, France

Three small French companies, Remy, Rousseau, and Thiebaud, merged, with aspirations of developing a full-line agricultural company. The heart of the CCM project was a tractor proposal, which was the reason for Deere & Company's interest in CCM. Deere's 51-percent ownership yielded a "green field" site factory in Orleans that began producing three- and four-cylinder engines for the factory in Mannheim.

Deere acquired 80 percent of the organization in 1962. It began producing some industrial equipment

This is the Funk Manufacturing, Inc., complex in Coffeyville, Kansas. Originally the Funk brothers manufactured airplanes. Deere & Company purchased the business in 1989 to provide power transmission equipment for Deere & Company products.

from components acquired from Dubuque, Iowa, which included industrial-type tractors.

The Remy factory in Senoche was closed in the 1970s, and forage harvester production was transferred to Ottumwa, Iowa, in the United States. Industrial equipment production ended in the early 1980s. In 1989, forage harvester production was transferred to Zweibrucken. The Orleans factory now produces only engines.

Lundell Limited
1961: Kent, England

Deere & Company purchased a majority interest in Lundell Limited, a small British manufacturer. The company's chief product was forage harvesters. The company's fate is unknown.

South African Cultivators (Proprietary) Limited
John Deere–Bobaas (Proprietary) Limited
John Deere (Proprietary) Limited
1962: Nigel, South Africa

Deere expanded into South Africa by purchasing 75 percent of South African Cultivators (Proprietary)

Limited. The firm had grown from a small farm equipment repair shop into an implement-manufacturing firm. When Deere acquired the company, annual sales were approximately $1,000,000. The company was renamed John Deere–Bobaas after the ownership change in 1962. In the late 1960s, the name was changed again to John Deere (Proprietary) Ltd.

Much of the 1970s and 1980s were characterized by the effect of apartheid. Deere steadfastly maintained its presence in South Africa during that period, believing that the jobs and opportunities given to locals was more important than leaving the country. Tractors were produced for a number of years until the late 1980s. Now only a line of planters is produced there.

Compagnie Française John Deere
1963: Suran, France

Compagnie Française John Deere and Etablissements R. Rousseau officially merged into one corporation on June 30, 1965. This new corporation carried the name Compagnie Française John Deere. This entity became the marketing arm for John Deere in France. Saran and

Orleans were adjacent cities located one hour south of Paris that share the same physical address.

John Deere Iberica
1967: Getafe, Spain

Ricardo Medem founded the factory in Getafe in 1953. Lanz owned 8 percent of the Spanish company at the time Deere acquired Lanz. Lanz products were built there, and Deere acquired controlling interest in 1967.

Tractors for the Spanish market were produced there until the early 1980s. Spain's membership in the European Union (EU) removed barriers to importing tractors, and the economic advantage of local production disappeared.

By the late 1980s, only a few tractors were produced at Getafe. These tractors were targeted at the orchard and vineyard market in Spain. All tractor production ended in the mid-1990s. Today, Getafe produces gears, gearboxes, and transmissions for Deere & Company products worldwide.

Chamberlain Industries
Chamberlain John Deere Proprietary, Ltd.
John Deere Ltd.
1970: Perth, Australia

Deere joined in partnership with Chamberlain Industries, purchasing a stock interest of approximately

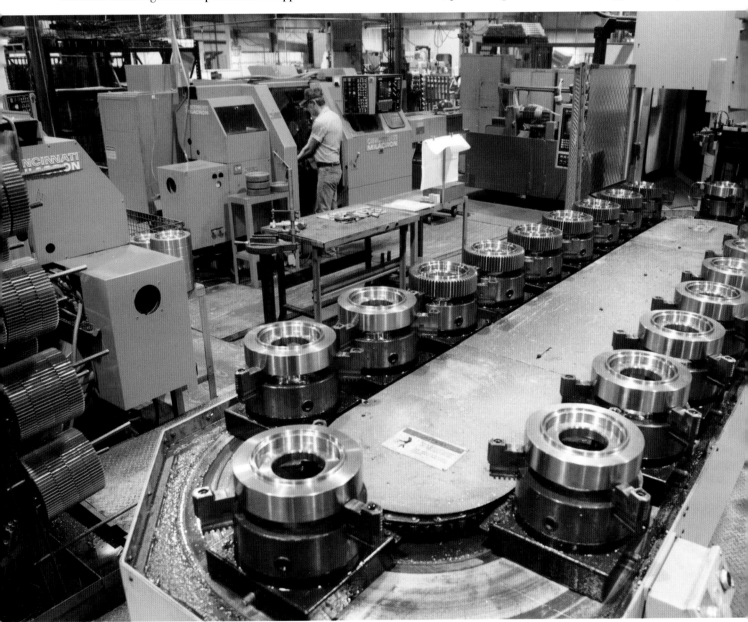

Here's part of the manufacturing operation at Funk Manufacturing, Inc. This 1990 photograph shows transmission parts being machined.

Combine harvesters and forage equipment are manufactured at this Zweibrucken, Germany, location.

29 percent in Chamberlain. Over a period of six years, Deere & Company's interest reached 49 percent.

The name was changed from Chamberlain Industries to Chamberlain John Deere Proprietary, Ltd. Chamberlain continued to manufacture and distribute its own products in Australia as well as manufacture certain John Deere products to be distributed by Chamberlain.

A munitions factory at Welschpool was used as a production facility for building planting equipment and implements for the Australian market. The Welschpool factory was sold in 1992 and continued to produce implements under license for Deere & Company.

The remaining Chamberlain–Deere & Company relationship was absorbed in what became the John Deere Ltd. business. The head office was moved from Perth, West Australia, to Brisbane, Queensland.

Today, John Deere Ltd. has parts warehouses in Perth, Melbourne, and Brisbane. Administrative offices are located in Brisbane. An office in Sydney manages loose engine sales.

European Parts Distribution Center
1983: Bruchsal, Germany

The Bruchsal site is located 45 kilometers from Mannheim. There are three facilities on the site. The European Parts Distribution Center (EPDC) is the central parts warehouse and distribution center for Deere's European operations.

The EPDC expanded in 1985 and again in 1990. This facility stocks 115,000 parts in three pallet/bin/miniload high rises with roughly 140,000 locations in 14 aisles, altogether 40,4000 square meters.

Here's a 1966 aerial view of the John Deere Werke in Mannheim, Germany. Founded in 1859, the Lanz company produced stationary steam engines and the Bulldog tractor. Today the Mannheim facility produces John Deere agricultural tractors.

The EPDC runs in two shifts and employs 140 people.

Also at the Bruchsal site is a cab manufacturing facility. The cabs produced at Bruchsal are used by Mannheim for tractors and by Zweibrucken for combines and self-propelled forage harvesters. The Bruchsal factory is part of the Mannheim factory management organization.

In 1990, a European training facility was built at the Bruchsal site. This training facility supports dealers throughout the European Union (EU) and the Commonwealth of Independent States(CIS). The previous training facility was located at the Mannheim factory.

SABO
1990: Gummersbach, Germany

This factory was purchased as an entry into the consumer products market in Europe. The company produces walk-behind mowers for Europe.

Roberine
1991: Enschede, The Netherlands

This factory was purchased to complement the company's commercial turf care products for Europe.

Mortores John Deere
1998: Torreon, Mexico

This factory was built to produce Deere's engines for use in North America. It has additional production capacity to supplement engine production at the Waterloo and Dubuque plants.

AFFLIATED COMPANYS

John Deere S.A. De C.V.
Industrias John Deere
1955: Mexico City, Mexico

Deere & Company opened a sales office. This initial entry into the market led Deere to believe local manufacturing would be advantageous.

1959: Monterrey, Mexico

A new factory was opened. Previously the plant was operated in rented facilities. Initial products were tractor assembly and implements.

1984: Saltillo, Mexico

At the Mannheim, Germany, Tractor Assembly facility the right cab, or enclosures, arrives at the proper time for installation. Again, the computerized overhead delivery system makes it all possible.

Deere & Company's John Deere (Proprietary) Limited facility is in Nigel, South Africa. Tractors were produced here for a number of years, ceasing in the late 1980s. Today it's the site of planter production.

Deere & Company purchased the old International Harvester factory in the late 1970s. Tractor production was moved from Monterrey to Saltillo. Excavator production was added in 1996.

1996: Chihuahua, Mexico

This facility was brought on-line to produce axles for OEM customers and the Construction Equipment Manufacturing division. In 1996, Deere & Company purchased the outstanding 49 percent of the Monterrey-Saltillo Company. All the entities have been consolidated into a holding company: Industrias John Deere (IJD).

John Deere Intercontinental, Ltd.
John Deere Intercontinental, GmbH.
1961

Deere & Company's international structure was reorganized. The Venezuelan holding company, John Deere Intercontinental, S.A. was dissolved and a new Canadian company, John Deere Intercontinental, Ltd., was formed.

John Deere Intercontinental, GmbH was a sales branch organization for countries that didn't have a local John Deere manufacturing or sales branch operation. The office was located in Moline, Illinois. Due to changes in tax treaties between the United States and other countries, the country of incorporation moved from Bermuda (Ltd.) to Germany (GmbH) in the early 1980s. This sales branch was responsible for the dealers and distributors in Latin America and Asia.

In 1997, the office in Moline was disbanded, and dealer and distributor management for various countries was transferred to regional offices in Latin America and Asia.

In general, the overseas organization has been evolving throughout the period since the 1956 purchase of Lanz to today. Other manufacturing sites have emerged and disappeared over the years, including the manufacture of tractors in Turkey in the 1970s, Venezuela in the 1970s, and combines and balers in Iran in the 1970s.

SLC S.A. Industria e Comercio

This Deere & Company factory in Monterey, Mexico, was opened in 1959. Originally the facility's products were tractor assembly and implements. In the late 1970s, tractor production was moved to the old International Harvester factory in Satillo that had been purchased by Deere. Today the Monterey plant produces tillage tools and cultivating equipment.

SLC–John Deere
1976: Horizontina, Brazil

Deere & Company contacted Schneider, Logemann & Cia, Ltd. about possible collaboration in the manufacture of combines. Schneider-Logemann (SL) is a family-run company located in Horizontina, Rio Grande de Sul. SL had been producing a combine or harvesting machine for local market use since 1945 and had a good name in the local market. In addition, SL had a substantial farming operation in Brazil, with the first farm acquired in 1957.

In 1977, Deere & Company and SL formed a joint venture agreement called SLC for the manufacture of combines. SLC was 20 percent owned by Deere, 80 percent owned by Schneider, Logemann & Cia, Ltd. Deere also injected combine technology from its Zweibrucken

factory. A new factory was built in 1989. Today, it is recognized as a state-of-the-art facility.

By 1996, SLC commanded a 40-percent market share in the Brazilian market, and it was exporting to Deere & Company in Argentina as well as Deere & Company dealers throughout South America.

In 1996, Deere & Company concluded negotiations to acquire an additional 20 percent of the company, which was renamed SLC–John Deere. It recognized a stronger relationship with Deere & Company and gained further recognition of the Deere & Company name in Brazil.

At the same time, tractor production began at the Horizontina factory. These tractors are local market adaptations of Deere & Company's 5000, 6000, and 7000 models produced in the United States and

This 1920 image of the chemistry laboratory at the Union Malleable Iron Company in East Moline, Illinois, is a sharp contrast to the present "lab" facilities at the Waterloo Foundry.

A Coordinate Measuring Machine (CMM) at the Waterloo Foundry checks a casting for proper tolerances. This evaluation room and its equipment highlight the great advancements made in technology since the lab at the Union Malleable Iron Company was built in 1920.

Germany. These tractors are also exported to Argentina and the rest of South America.

Tuff-Torq
1977

Deere & Company and Yanmar, which owns Tuff-Torq, signed a design joint venture agreement, but no manufacturing entity is attached to the relationship. Deere & Company has had a long relationship with Yanmar, which included purchase of products and components. Yanmar has a garden tractor transmission manufacturing factory. Deere & Company has a minority equity position in Tuff-Torq, a U.S. company.

Deere-Hitachi Construction Machinery Corporation
1988: Kernersville, North Carolina

In 1963, Deere & Company explored a licensing agreement with Hitachi for manufacturing and sales. The two companies couldn't reach a workable agreement and in 1970 terminated the venture. However, a successful joint venture was entered into in the 1980s to produce components for hydraulic excavators. Initial production was large weldments for the boom and arms of excavators.

Cameco do Brazil
1997: Catalao, Brazil

In 1997, Deere & Company purchased 49 percent of the sugarcane harvesting equipment manufacturer Cameco located in Thibodaux. In 1998, Deere and Cameco broke ground for a sugarcane harvester production facility in Catalao, Goias, in central Brazil. Cameco do Brazil also has a sales office in Ribero Preto, Sao Paulo.

INDEX